AMERICAN QUAKERS TODAY

•

AMERICAN QUAKERS TODAY

•

Edwin B. Bronner, *Editor*

•

1966

Friends World Committee,
American Section and Fellowship Council

152-A North Fifteenth Street
Philadelphia, Pennsylvania   19102

Cover Design by William B. Kriebel

•

Printed in the United States of America
by Sowers Printing Company, Lebanon, Pennsylvania

INTRODUCTION

IN THE SUMMER of 1964, shortly after sharing in the first *ad hoc* committee meeting to plan for the Fourth World Conference at Guilford in 1967, I participated in a Quaker Pilgrimage in the Northwest Country of England. One afternoon during our week together we gathered at the Kendal meetinghouse where I was asked to give a lecture describing American Quakerism today.

It was apparent from the questions which were asked at the end of the lecture that there was a great deal of interest in American Quakerism, especially in the differences which exist between various groups, and that very little was known about Friends in North America. With a World Conference coming soon, and with the hope that Friends would travel around and visit among Friends while in the United States, it seemed desirable to prepare a publication for visitors to read. It may be assumed that many Americans will also find such a volume informative and useful.

The first chapter attempts to explain why and how American Friends came to be divided into many yearly meetings and why they appear to differ from one another in many ways. It also traces some of the steps taken toward greater unity in recent years. This brief explanation is obviously incomplete, and is supplemented by some suggested reading and a diagram to indicate in a simple fashion the history of the changes. The author is indebted to Henry J. Cadbury, T. Canby Jones, and Marshall O. Sutton for reading this chapter and making suggestions and offering criticism.

In asking each of the authors of the next five chapters to

5

write about his or her particular group of Friends, I wrote the following:

> "We would like each writer to emphasize the positive, to stress the contributions which are being made by the part of Quakerism which he or she represents. We would like something about the basic emphasis, something about the present concerns, and the directions in which the particular group of Friends are moving. As the visitors to the United States move from one yearly meeting to another, they will find many things in common. However, they will also recognize differences, and we would like to make it easier for the visitors to understand these differences through reading your essay."

These five authors wrote as individuals, and not as official spokesmen for their groups, even though some hold official positions.

The final chapter attempts to summarize some other aspects of American Quakerism. The description of the American Friends Service Committee was provided by the Information Service of that body. There are other organizations such as the Young Friends of North America, the Friends Historical Association, and the Friends Council on Education which have not been described here. They are all listed in the *Handbook of the Religious Society of Friends*, a publication which is used constantly by those wishing to learn more about Friends, along with the *Friends Directory*, published every two years by the FWCC.

It is with deep appreciation that I acknowledge the assistance received from several persons. William B. Kriebel has been responsible for all of the art work needed in connection with the publication. The entire manuscript was read by Blanche C. Shaffer, Herbert M. Hadley, and James F. Walker, and they made many valuable suggestions. Mary Hoxie Jones has assisted in the proofreading.

This modest publication has been gathered together in order to help Friends to know and understand one another. While it indicates that all groups of Friends have much in common, no attempt has been made to gloss over differences which exist. We hope and pray that through greater knowledge and understanding it will be possible for all Friends to love and appreciate one another, even while cherishing those things which are distinctive in each group.

EDWIN B. BRONNER

Haverford College
Haverford, Pennsylvania
September, 1965

CONTENTS

• 1 •

AN HISTORICAL SUMMARY
by Edwin B. Bronner

THE VARIETY WITHIN QUAKERISM in the United States must seem most confusing to a person looking at it for the first time. If he settles in Washington, D.C., he soon learns that there are two Baltimore Yearly Meetings, and that each of them belongs to a larger organization, one called the Friends United Meeting, and the other, the Friends General Conference. When visiting in North Carolina during the Fourth Friends World Conference in 1967, he finds that most Friends are in North Carolina Yearly Meeting which is a part of Friends United Meeting,[1] but there are other Friends in North Carolina Yearly Meeting (Conservative), and still others who are a part of Ohio Yearly Meeting (Evangelical).

If a visitor goes to Ohio he finds that there are five distinct yearly meetings in that one state which represent the five different types of Friends described in this publication. Altogether there are twenty-six yearly meetings in the United States, plus a number of independent meetings without a yearly meeting affiliation, with a grand total of 120,000 members. All of this is sometimes confusing to American Friends who live in the midst of this condition, but it must seem almost impossible to Quakers from other parts of the globe.

If one takes a quick glance at Quakers around the world

---

[1] Formerly Five Years Meeting.

it is apparent that the prevailing pattern is to form a yearly meeting in a nation when there are enough members of the Religious Society of Friends in one geographical area to make this a useful and meaningful step.

Continental European Friends have formed seven separate yearly meetings, even though they total less than 1,200 persons, and nearly one-half of that number are in Germany. Norway, Sweden, and Denmark each has a separate yearly meeting, even though altogether there are less than 300 Quakers in these Scandinavian countries for they believe that these separate organizations serve a useful function.

There are exceptions to this general rule. German Friends are determined to maintain one single yearly meeting even though a part of their members live in the German Democratic Republic, and the larger number are in the German Federal Republic. Irish Friends have continued to meet as one Ireland Yearly Meeting despite the fact that Ulster Quarterly Meeting is in Northern Ireland, a part of the United Kingdom, and Leinster and Munster Quarterly Meetings are in Eire or the Irish Republic. While the vast majority of the Friends in East Africa Yearly Meeting are in Kenya, the yearly meeting does include Quakers of Uganda and Tanzania as well. Southern Africa Yearly Meeting also embraces members from more than one nation.

It is noteworthy that British Friends have maintained a single yearly meeting, with only minor exceptions, for more than three centuries, despite the difficulties of travel in the earlier days, and the social, cultural and economic differences which have always existed within the yearly meeting. For example, the rural Quaker of the north country was very different from the London Friend, and the Scottish or Welsh Quaker often must have felt himself to be distinctive within London Yearly Meeting. There have been theological differences ever since the seventeenth century, but most of these differences have been overcome by a strong pervasive feeling of unity. The Beaconite controversy led to the formation of a separate group which called itself the Evangelical Friends in the 1830's, but it soon disappeared as the dissidents joined other denominations. It is true that today there is still a remnant of Fritchley General Meeting, which was formed in 1869, but aside from this exception, all British Friends are united in one body with more than 21,000 members.

Friends in North America have been divided from the very beginning. The Quakers of New England began to hold General Meetings in 1661, and reckon their history from that date. This would make New England Yearly Meeting seven years older than London Yearly Meeting, established in 1668, a claim which outrages some British Friends, but amuses others. However, it is typical of American efforts to push their beginnings back as far as possible in order to gain an appearance of antiquity.

During the rest of the seventeenth century five other yearly meetings were created. Philadelphia Yearly Meeting, which included Friends in West New Jersey and Delaware, as well as Pennsylvania, was established in 1681, and embraced several thousand Quakers before 1700. Between Philadelphia and New England the Friends of New York, and especially of Long Island, separated from New England and formed New York Yearly Meeting. South of Penn's colony the Friends established yearly meetings in Maryland, Virginia, and the Carolinas. Maryland Yearly Meeting changed its name to Baltimore, and Virginia Yearly Meeting ceased to exist in 1843 when it became a quarterly meeting under Baltimore.

There were good reasons for the creation of six separate yearly meetings in the English colonies. The distance between the different provinces was the most obvious reason. It was more than 800 miles by sea from Providence, Rhode

Island, to Charleston, South Carolina, and more than 1,000 miles by land. Roads were virtually non-existent until near the middle of the eighteenth century. There were no regular coaches, inns were few in number and food and housing in such places was indescribable. While individual Quaker ministers travelled from place to place to worship with Friends and minister to them, it was impossible for large numbers of Friends to travel from one colony to another for yearly meetings.

The inhabitants of the various colonies had little in common with one another. Some were governed under proprietary charters, a few were virtually self-governing, and others were ruled by Royal Governors. The emphasis was on tobacco in Maryland, Virginia, and the Carolinas. In Philadelphia Yearly Meeting there was a mixture of men in farming and in mercantile pursuits. Long Island farmers were predominant in New York Yearly Meeting, while shipping and mercantile occupations were dominant in New England.

Quakers, like all colonists, looked to England more than toward neighboring colonies. Frequently it was easier to get from a colonial port to Britain than to travel from one coastal port to another. While the American yearly meetings were in communication with one another, they were closer to London Yearly Meeting than to the others along the Atlantic coast.

Friends did not have a printer available, except in Philadelphia, until the second quarter of the eighteenth century. They continued to depend upon the publications of London Yearly Meeting long after that date, for Philadelphia made no effort to become the publishing headquarters for American Quakerism.

It is clear that in the colonial period it was necessary for Friends to organize separate yearly meetings in the several regions of the colonies. No new yearly meeting was created until 1813 when the westward movement led to the establishment of Ohio Yearly Meeting, followed by Indiana in 1821.

The Separations

The establishment of eight yearly meetings by 1821 as the result of conditions which were largely geographical in nature, is one aspect of the complex picture of American Quakerism. Later in the 1820's separations within existing yearly meetings began to develop, and these have continued to the present, with the latest schism in 1957 when a large part of the membership of Nebraska Yearly Meeting withdrew to form Rocky Mountain Yearly Meeting.

Through the years there were several schisms in the Society of Friends. The John Perrot separation had come in the 1660's, followed by the Wilkinson-Story controversy in the next decade. The Keithian Schism had developed in Philadelphia Yearly Meeting in the 1690's, and spread back to London. Several hundred Friends who joined the patriot's cause in the American War for Independence had later organized the Free Quaker movement which lasted until 1836. There was a serious controversy among Irish Friends in the 1790's, and New England Friends went through a trying period just before the Great Separation of 1827.

It was also true that churches in the United States were frequently split by differences over doctrine or political beliefs. During the "Great Awakening" in the colonial period, the Presbyterians and Congregationalists were divided between those who embraced the new ideas and those who held to a more traditional viewpoint. New denominations sprang into being whenever a religious leader believed he had discovered a new truth and was able to gather a band of devoted followers around him. Several major denominations split into northern and southern branches over the slavery question. The religious toleration which was widely accepted in the United States by the late eighteenth cen-

tury not only made provision for a variety of religious denominations, but virtually encouraged the creation of new
churches. Thus there was ample precedent for the separation of 1827.

In the United States the Society of Friends went through
a low period in the first quarter of the nineteenth century.
That spiritual life was at a low ebb is reflected in the
journals of such Friends as Stephen Grellet, Thomas Shillitoe, and Job Scott. The educational level of Friends was
also deficient. Too few Friends received even an average
education and virtually none received the best education
available. Instead of maintaining the searching, the openness to new revelations of the first generation of Friends,
there was a tendency to draw inward, to rely upon tradition, or upon the letter rather than the spirit. Friends
placed their faith in authority, in what had been revealed
as truth to previous generations instead of remaining flexible and open to new revelations, to the Spirit of Christ,
or what some called the Inward Light.

Even now it is difficult to obtain a clear picture of what
was taking place in the Society at that time. Friends were
not loath to publish statements explaining their position
and denouncing their opponents, but such statements cannot always be accepted at face value. For example, the
Orthodox Friends insisted that the Hicksite branch denied
the divinity of Christ, the doctrine of the atonement and
the divine inspiration of the Scriptures. The Hicksite bodies protested that these accusations were untrue, and their
Books of Discipline bear out their statements.[2]

Even though Friends had withdrawn from society in

---

[2] The terms "Orthodox" and "Hicksite" will be used for the two
branches until 1902, by which time both the Five Years Meeting and
the Friends General Conference had been formed. Some authors have
used the word "liberal" instead of "Hicksite," but in the early years
after the Separation, this term is not entirely appropriate.

large measure after the trials of the years beginning with the French and Indian War (1754-1763), they were not impervious to the new ideas and schools of thought which whirled about them. The democratic ideas enunciated in the Declaration of Independence, and the spirit which grew out of the French Revolution had a profound influence on Americans. Younger Friends responded, and began to look for reflections of these beliefs within the Religious Society of Friends. At a time when the Elders were very powerful in Friends meetings, there was little room for this new democratic spirit.

Hand in hand with the democratic spirit were the philosophical ideas of the French Revolution, the spirit of rationalism, of deism, a new and more liberal religious philosophy. Religious liberalism might have taken hold in Quakerism over a period of time if it had not run head on into a second religious movement of this period, evangelicalism. At the time when religious liberalism reinforced some aspects of Quakerism, evangelical beliefs strengthened opposing tendencies.

Religious liberalism strengthened the Quaker opposition to creeds, but carried this tendency to the point where it was scarcely necessary to believe anything in order to be a Quaker. The Evangelical movement on the other hand led to an insistence on acceptance of certain fundamental beliefs, and demanded condemnation of all who failed to embrace every tenet of the evangelical position. Thus the liberal element became more tolerant of all varieties of positions at the very moment when the evangelical wing became most intolerant of any deviation.

It is clear that at least in Philadelphia Yearly Meeting there was a tendency of the country Quakers to be estranged from the city Friends. When the schism came, more than two-thirds of the country Friends joined the so-called Hicksite group and more than two-thirds of the city

Quakers embraced the orthodox group. Some observers find that the Orthodox represented the wealthy conservative Friends, and the other branch represented the Jasksonian democratic spirit of the day.

Elias Hicks (1748-1830) was regarded as the leader of those who were unwilling to accept things as they were, who began to ask for more freedom on the one hand, and to resist what were regarded as evangelical innovations on the other. He lived on Long Island, at Jericho, farmed, and travelled in the ministry. He imbibed some of the rationalist and deist ideas of his day, but was also conservative in many ways. In his preaching against the doctrines of the Evangelical Friends, he believed that he was defending the true beliefs of the first Quakers, and especially their belief in the Inward Light. He had no desire to cause a schism in the Society of Friends, and never wished to be the leader of the part of the Society which carried his name.

It has been customary to place a good bit of the responsibility for the Separation of 1827 on English Quaker ministers who were travelling in America during the decade of the twenties. According to tradition, these British Friends, strongly evangelical in emphasis, went up and down the country preaching an undiluted evangelical Christianity which forced a showdown between the two elements in American Quakerism.

It is true that all of these visitors supported the wing which came to be called Orthodox, but they were not all evangelical. Thomas Shillitoe in particular, but also George and Ann Jones had not embraced the evangelical emphasis which had been taken over by some English Friends from Methodism. On the other hand, Anna Braithwaite, William Forster, Elizabeth Robson, Isaac Stephenson, and George Withy were evangelical in emphasis.

It is worth noting that there had been a pronounced decrease in intervisitation between British and American

Friends in the quarter century before the Separation. The Napoleonic Wars, and later the War of 1812 had virtually cut off all opportunities for travel back and forth across the Atlantic. Very few Friends had gone from Philadelphia, New York and Baltimore Yearly Meetings to live and travel among English Friends since 1800. Instead of voicing criticism of the British Friends who did come to America in these years, it might be better to express regret that there was not a great deal more intervisitation, with Friends travelling in both directions. This would have provided a broader base from which to judge changing conditions.

It is quite clear that the members of each group believed that they were defending the true beliefs of early Friends against attacks which were alien in origin. The Evangelical Friends believed that their opponents were infected with the new and dangerous teachings of the French rationalists. The followers of Hicks believed that the Evangelicals were advocating novel beliefs which had been absorbed from Methodism and Episcopalianism. Each group had seized a portion of the message of early Friends and rejected the rest, or at least the rest as they saw it interpreted by their opponents.

The first schism came in Philadelphia Yearly Meeting in 1827, and soon two-thirds of the membership formed a yearly meeting which was labelled "Hicksite," the remaining one-third were the "Orthodox." In the following year New York Yearly Meeting split along nearly the same lines, with the "Hicksites" in the majority. In Baltimore only a fraction were loyal to the "Orthodox" position, and the balance were Hicksite. The reverse was true in Indiana, where only a tiny group joined the Hicksite element. In Ohio Yearly Meeting the two groups were evenly divided. There were no separations in New England, North Carolina and Virginia Yearly Meetings.

London Yearly Meeting chose to recognize the Orthodox

yearly meetings and to ignore the Hicksite ones, a policy which it maintained until 1915. Distressed by what it considered the doctrinal unsoundness of this group, London Yearly Meeting revised its *Book of Discipline* in order to include stronger statements of Christian orthodoxy than had been issued previously.

Within the Orthodox branch of the Society a second schism began in the 1840's, and other splits along roughly the same lines of difference came as late as 1903.

Two tendencies began to be apparent within the Orthodox yearly meetings. One group seemed to become much like other Protestant sects in belief, although maintaining many Quaker testimonies and practices. The other group, although maintaining orthodox Christian beliefs, seemed to be increasingly attached to Quaker tradition; they were determined to preserve Friends' testimonies from any change or modification, and were especially concerned to protect the beliefs in the Inward Light. Joseph John Gurney (1788-1846) became the symbol of the first group, and they were called Gurneyites, in addition to continuing to carry the name Orthodox. The other group was led in the beginning by John Wilbur (1774-1856) and they were called Wilburites or Conservatives.

Gurney, scion of the Gurneys of Norwich, England, a man of great wealth and position, was a leading advocate of evangelical tendencies among English Friends, and was an internationally known Bible scholar widely read and quoted in America. He made a triumphal tour of the United States, beginning in 1837, and many Friends became enthusiastic supporters of his beliefs.

Wilbur, reared in modest circumstances in Hopkinton, Rhode Island, earned his living teaching school, and never enjoyed any pecuniary success, nor did he gain a large following. Wilbur first spoke out against Gurney while travelling in the ministry in Great Britain from 1831 to 1833, and frequently spoke against Gurney during the latter's travels in the United States.

John Wilbur continued to speak against Gurney, and against what he felt were undesirable tendencies in the Society. His yearly meeting feeling him to be troublesome and divisive, tried to labor with him. He refused to be silenced, and was disowned in 1843. Two years later some 500 New England Friends rallied around him to form a new yearly meeting, alongside the old New England Yearly Meeting with 6,500 members.

In 1854 in Ohio Yearly Meeting, the Gurneyite element, which was in the minority, separated itself from the majority which was sympathetic with the Wilburite tendencies. Philadelphia Yearly Meeting was sorely pressed by this action. Within the yearly meeting there was a division, and the Friends knew that if they recognized the Wilburite body it would lead to estrangement with other Orthodox yearly meetings. In order to avoid controversy, Philadelphia Yearly Meeting ceased communicating with all other yearly meetings, a policy which it maintained until after 1910.

Later in the 1870's new Conservative yearly meetings were set off in Iowa, Western (Indiana), and Kansas, as the Orthodox yearly meetings accepted the pastoral system, embraced revivalism and the use of music in worship, which caused minorities in these bodies to feel that they could only preserve Quaker principles by withdrawing. North Carolina (Conservative) was the last one formed, in 1903. Canada Yearly Meeting (Conservative) started in 1867.

The Pastoral Movement

Among the Gurneyite or Orthodox yearly meetings there was a positive response to the revival movement which swept over the Middle West area of the United States in

the years after the Civil War. Friends shared in revival
meetings, held them in their meetinghouses, and gained
many new members as a result. However, these new Quakers had not been trained in the unprogrammed way of
worship, they had no background and tradition to support
them, and Meetings soon realized that something needed
to be added to the prevailing pattern of worship and organization. Monthly Meetings began to hire the visiting
evangelist to stay on, or to pay a person to serve in a
pastoral capacity part time, or finally to hire a full time
minister, following the lead of the Protestant churches
around them. In the space of a generation most of the
mid-west yearly meetings adopted the pastoral system.

In addition to the continuation of extensive revivalistic
efforts in the communities in which they lived, Friends became deeply concerned about the need for missionary work
in many parts of the world. Missionaries were sent to Asia,
Africa, and Latin America. Although Philadelphia Yearly
Meeting participated in the missionary effort through work
in Japan, it was really more Wilburite than Gurneyite, despite the fact that it was called Orthodox, and it did not
embrace the pastoral system. Baltimore Yearly Meeting
(Orthodox) did not adopt the idea of a paid ministry, and
there were meetings in both New York and New England
Yearly Meetings which continued to meet on the basis of
silence. None of the Hicksite or Wilburite yearly meetings
turned to the pastoral system.

Among the pastoral Friends two tendencies began to
evolve. Some Yearly Meetings made a determined effort
to remain faithful to Quaker beliefs and testimonies, within the framework of the pastoral system. Such groups often
had periods of silent worship along with the sermon
preached by the pastor, and the music which had been
brought in by the revival movement. These Friends maintained a close relationship with London Yearly Meeting,

and began to gather together to strengthen one another. They first met in 1887 at Richmond, Indiana, and, meeting every five years thereafter, created the Five Years Meeting of Friends in 1902. There were more than 80,000 Friends in this body, in twelve yearly meetings. There was a good bit of variety represented in this new organization, ranging from fairly conservative, traditional Friends in Baltimore, New York and New England Yearly Meetings, to very evangelical Quakers from the middle west and far west. The Five Years Meeting, which now meets every three years and calls itself the Friends United Meeting, is the largest and most influential body of Quakers in America today. There is even more variation in belief and practice among its 67,000 members today than in 1902.

When the Five Years Meeting was formed, one Gurneyite yearly meeting refused to join on the grounds that the basis for membership was not sufficiently creedal. This was Ohio Yearly Meeting. Some members of that body were very concerned to emphasize literal adherence to the commands of Scripture even at the expense of Quaker beliefs and testimonies, to the point of advocating baptism and communion. Later two other yearly meetings left the Five Years Meeting: Oregon Yearly Meeting in 1926, and Kansas Yearly Meeting in 1937. They feared the "liberalism" they saw in the Five Years Meeting, and believed that it would compromise their Christian witness if they continued to participate in its program and objectives. Two other bodies with similar concerns have separated from existing yearly meetings. In 1926 Central Yearly Meeting was created in Indiana by Friends who had belonged to Indiana and Western Yearly Meetings. This body does not have fellowship with any other group of Friends. In 1957 Rocky Mountain Yearly Meeting separated from Nebraska Yearly Meeting. The latter cooperates with Ohio, Oregon, and Kansas Yearly Meetings.

These evangelical yearly meetings carry on extensive missionary work in many parts of the world, they maintain liberal arts colleges with a strong Christian emphasis, publish periodicals, and conduct other extensive activities. Their members formed the nucleus of the Evangelical Association of Friends, organized in 1947, although members of other yearly meetings have also been active. In 1963 the Evangelical Friends Alliance was formed by Ohio, Oregon, Kansas and Rocky Mountain Yearly Meetings.

Until very recently Conservative or Wilburite yearly meetings made little effort to work together. For many years these Friends had few contacts with Friends of the other branches, and only occasionally visited one another, although they did correspond with one another. However, in 1965 Conservative Friends all met together for a conference at Barnesville, Ohio. Two of the Conservative yearly meetings, Western and Kansas, have disappeared, and only Ohio, Iowa, and North Carolina exist today. Together they have a membership of less than 2,000.

The Friends in the yearly meetings labelled Hicksite began to gather together informally as early as 1868 when they organized the First-day School Conference. Other committees cutting across yearly meeting lines were formed in the years that followed, such as the Friends Union of Philanthropic Labor. In 1900 four of these associations decided to organize a Friends General Conference, and the members of the seven yearly meetings have been referred to as General Conference Friends since that time. This was a very loose organization, with the Conference having no power or authority over the yearly meetings. In 1902 Philadelphia Yearly Meeting made up one-half of the 22,000 members, with New York, Baltimore, Indiana, Illinois, Genesee (Canada) and Ohio making up the other half. Ohio Yearly Meeting has since merged with Indiana.

Twentieth Century Developments

There are other developments in the twentieth century which claim our attention and interest. The creation of the American Friends Service Committee in 1917, and the establishment of the Friends Committee on National Legislation in 1943 are both important developments which will be discussed in a later chapter. In addition to the formation of the Five Years Meeting within the Orthodox wing, and the Friends General Conference in the Hicksite part of the Society, a third unifying tendency began to evolve. Monthly meetings, quarterly meetings, and then yearly meetings from the different branches began to join to form united meetings. After World War I a new development evolved when unaffiliated or independent meetings began to spring up across the nation: meetings with no connection to existing bodies of Friends. Unity was fostered both by creating new independent meetings and through the organic union of existing bodies.

In the twentieth century, and especially after World War I, Friends realized that many of the differences which led to the separations of the nineteenth century were fading. Regretting the divisions of an earlier generation, and recognizing that many of the divisions were no longer important, Friends began to look for ways to come back together.

They discovered that there were often as many differences within one branch of the Society of Friends as there were between two branches. Friends were spread widely across the theological spectrum within a General Conference yearly meeting, as well as within Orthodox yearly meetings. Also, as Friends worked together for peace, and especially through the American Friends Service Committee, and learned to know and love one another, they began to feel that they should be united once more. The

Friends of what is now the Evangelical Friends Alliance have not shared in this movement to any degree, but they have taken unifying steps within their own wing of Quakerism. The Conservative Friends were slow to accept the idea of working with other Quakers, but eventually both the Canadian and the New England Conservative yearly meetings were merged with other groups in their regions. More recently, Ohio Yearly Meeting (Barnesville) has cooperated with the Committee on Greater Unity in the Ohio-Michigan area, and Iowa Yearly Meeting has welcomed new monthly meetings into its fellowship which were formerly independent meetings under the sponsorship of the Friends World Committee, American Section. Both Iowa Yearly Meeting and North Carolina Yearly Meeting share in many joint ventures, especially the work of the American Friends Service Committee and the Friends Committee on National Legislation, but have not made any effort to merge with other groups.

Young Friends were among the earliest to urge all branches of Friends to work together, learn to know one another, and eventually to join into single bodies. Young Friends began to hold joint conferences in 1910, and this effort has continued through the decades. The Young Friends of the two Philadelphia Yearly Meetings began to work together, and insisted that they were one body long before the two yearly meetings were united. Today the body known as the Young Friends of North America includes participants from every shade of belief and practice.

As the American population became more mobile in the years after World War I, because of the automobile, new business practices, and other influences, Friends frequently found themselves living in areas where there had formerly been no Friends. In an earlier period Quakers were critical of members who went off to live where there was no organized meeting, and this was sometimes cause for disownment. However, in the twentieth century Friends decided that they should encourage and assist those who were isolated, and hoped that such persons would become the nucleus for a new meeting.

The Friends who went to live in areas where there was no local Meeting tended to gather in academic communities, although this was not always true. These persons often found students in colleges and universities who responded to the Quaker worship and way of life. In addition, a number of young people who had worked with the American Friends Service Committee wanted to continue their Quaker connections when they returned to their homes or colleges, and joined these groups. Soon there were many of these worship groups across the nation. They contained members of many different yearly meetings as well as persons who had not been Quakers before. Often a local meeting contained Friends from two or three different branches of the Society, and they found in the new situation that their common heritage and belief were stronger than the institutional differences of the branches.

As these meetings were not under the care of any yearly meeting, they turned to the one Quaker organization which cut across lines and had a national outlook, the American Friends Service Committee. A special committee, called the Fellowship Committee was set up to assist these new meetings. Eventually this became a separate body named the American Friends Fellowship Council. Because meetings wanted to be able to supervise marriages, Friends wanted to move their membership from their old meetings to the new one, and convinced Friends wanted to join the new meetings, the Fellowship Council decided it should take on the responsibility of recognizing Monthly Meetings, in order to make it possible for Friends in these new groups to perform these tasks. The first of these monthly meetings was the one in Cleveland, Ohio, recognized in

1936. In response to the desire of many persons who had strong ties to some other denomination, but wanted to maintain some relationship with the Society of Friends, the Wider Quaker Fellowship was also created by the Fellowship Council. Today there are nearly 4,000 Wider Quaker Fellows. Often they worship with local meetings, and sometimes they join the Society of Friends. In 1954 the Fellowship Council was merged with the American Section of the Friends World Committee for Consultation.

Four new yearly meetings have developed largely as the result of the growth of these new meetings. They are Pacific Yearly Meeting, 1947; South Central Yearly Meeting, 1961; Southeastern Yearly Meeting, 1962; and Lake Erie Yearly Meeting in 1963. In addition there are two associations of Friends meetings, the Southern Appalachian Association, and the Missouri Valley Conference. There are also a number of individual monthly meetings and worship groups which are associated with the American Section, FWCC. They, like all Friends Meetings in the United States, are listed in *Friends Directory, Meetings for Worship in the United States and Canada,* published biennially by the American Section, FWCC.

The other tendency toward the uniting of the different groups of Friends began at the local meeting level. The 57th Street Meeting in Chicago joined both Western and Illinois Yearly Meetings, the Chestnut Hill Meeting joined both the Arch and Race Street yearly meetings in Philadelphia, the familiar names of the Orthodox and Hicksite bodies, and there were soon others.

In 1945 the Friends of New England joined to form New England Yearly Meeting, which included the Orthodox yearly meeting, the Wilburite body, and two independent meetings. The united yearly meeting maintained the membership in the Five Years Meeting which the Orthodox Friends held, and has since joined the Friends General

Conference. The various bodies in Canada joined together in 1955 to form the Canadian Yearly Meeting which belongs to both the Friends General Conference and the Five Years Meeting, now called the Friends United Meeting. In the same year the two New York yearly meetings joined together, and the united group maintained its membership in both bodies. The two Philadelphia yearly meetings also became a single body in 1955, and continued participation in the Friends General Conference. Arch Street Friends (Orthodox), had not belonged to the Five Years Meeting.

Thus there has been a pattern of Friends healing the differences of the nineteenth century and coming back into organic union with one another. It should be added that the two Baltimore yearly meetings are also working toward that goal. In other situations there is little or no attempt to achieve organic union, but fellowship together has increased. In the middle west this spirit has been implemented by the Committee on Greater Unity.

The uniting of yearly meetings has not decreased the total number because new bodies have been created where there were very few Friends before, or in regions where a separate approach to Quaker worship seemed desirable. Thus there are now twenty-seven yearly meetings in the United States and Canada. Most of these bodies fill a distinct need for the Friends they serve, although there may be more mergers in the years to come. The majority of the yearly meetings work together in harmony to fulfill their purpose for God and the Society of Friends.

References for Additional Reading

Grubb, Edward, *Separations, Their Causes and Effects* (London, 1914).

Jones, Rufus M., *The Later Periods of Quakerism*, 2 vol. (London, 1921).

Leach, Robert, *The Yearly Meetings of the Religious Society of Friends* (Pendle Hill, 1944).

Russell, Elbert, *The Separation After a Century* ([Philadelphia], 1928).

————, *The History of Quakerism* (New York, 1942).

Thomas, Allen C., and Richard H. Thomas, *A History of the Friends in America*, revised edit. (Philadelphia, 1930).

Williams, Walter R., *The Rich Heritage of Quakerism* (Grand Rapids, Mich., 1962).

Handbook of the Religious Society of Friends (Philadelphia, 1935, and subsequent years).

Trends in American and Canadian Quakerism, 1925-1950 (London, 1951).

Articles in *The* [Philadelphia] *Friend, Friends Intelligencer* (merged into *Friends Journal* in 1955), and the *American Friend* (changed to *Quaker Life* in 1960).

Articles in *Encyclopedia Britannica:* "Friends, Society of;" and *Book of the Year,* "Religion, Religious Society of Friends."

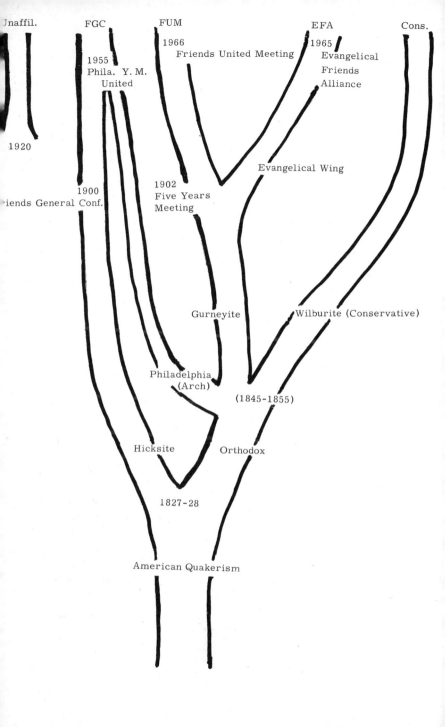

Unaffil.   FGC   FUM   EFA   Cons.

1966
Friends United Meeting

1965
Evangelical
Friends
Alliance

1955
Phila. Y. M.
United

1920

Evangelical Wing

1900
Friends General Conf.

1902
Five Years
Meeting

Gurneyite   Wilburite (Conservative)

Philadelphia
(Arch)

(1845-1855)

Hicksite   Orthodox

1827-28

American Quakerism

• 2 •

FRIENDS UNITED MEETING*
by David O. Stanfield

THE FRIENDS UNITED MEETING became the new name in 1965 for that world-wide fellowship of Friends formerly known as the Five Years Meeting of Friends. Two compelling reasons called for the change. First, the gathering of its representatives for worship and business began meeting at three year rather than at five year intervals. Secondly, the former name was puzzling to persons not acquainted with Quaker terminology. Below are outlined some of the reasons for adopting the new name.

Friends—As the followers of George Fox in the 17th century England came to have a common identity, they called themselves "Friends of Truth," suggesting a non-compromising acceptance of Divinely revealed truth as they experienced it individually and in corporate worship. "Ye are my friends, if ye do whatsoever I command you" (John 15:14) also became the basis for using "Friends" as their identification. The label "Quaker" was first used as a derogatory nickname because early Friends had called their hearers under a guilty conscience to quake or tremble under the power of God. This label is now often used by Friends. "Quakerism" indicates the way of life—in faith and practice—which Friends try to follow.

United—In recent years much progress has been made to unite Friends groups that were separated by geographical

---

* This chapter has been published separately as a pamphlet.

32

and theological divisions. The spirit of understanding and co-operation has been greatly advanced by the common interests and work found within the framework of Friends United Meeting's United Services program. The term "united" also suggests that Friends grow in fellowship as they become "united in the Lord," through their commitment to Him and His Way.

Meeting—This is a characteristically Quaker term suggesting that any gathering of Friends seeks to become a meeting in the presence of the Lord and in fellowship with one another. Friends feel that the term "church" should be reserved to describe the fellowship of believers in the living Christ—whoever they be or wherever they are. The church is more than a building or institution. The total fellowship of Friends is known, therefore, as "The Religious Society of Friends."

The local meeting (congregation) meets weekly for worship. Members of a local meeting meet each month for business; this is called the Monthly Meeting for business. Decisions are reached by the members on the basis of a corporate sense of leading by the Holy Spirit in keeping with the Scriptures. Business meetings use the services of a Presiding Clerk and a Recording Clerk. The local meeting gives to and accepts from larger bodies of Friends counsel and guidance. The organizational relationship is non-authoritarian.

Monthly Meetings in the same vicinity may hold joint meetings every three months for inspiration, fellowship and business. This gathering is called Quarterly Meeting.

The Quarterly Meetings in a larger region (sometimes covering one or more States) gather annually as a Yearly Meeting, similar to the Annual Conference, or Synod of other denominations.

Fourteen Yearly Meetings in the Americas and Africa have banded together to form the Friends United Meeting, representing over 103,000 members, or more than half the Friends in the world.

The Friends United Meeting gives expression to the corporateness of the body of Christ in its mission in the world. It is a body to which has been granted certain powers, and therefore, is more than a conference or loose federation.

The Friends United Meeting gathers every three years with about two hundred official representatives from its member-Yearly Meetings, fraternal representatives from other Yearly Meetings, and hundreds of other Friends from many parts of the world. These triennial sessions are occasions for inspiration, future planning and business.

How Did the Friends United Meeting Come To Be?

In the 1650's in England thousands of religious "seekers," dissatisfied with the formalism and spiritual lethargy of the Church of their day, responded to George Fox's ministry which declared that the living Christ had come to teach His people Himself. These seekers became finders of a satisfying spiritual way of life based on a first-hand experience of God, mediated not by clergy or ritual but by the immediate presence of the living Christ.

In colonial America many Friends made significant contributions to the emerging United States. They played major roles in leadership in the colonies of Pennsylvania, New Jersey, Rhode Island, Maryland and North Carolina. As the Ohio Territory opened up many Friends on the Eastern Seaboard migrated westward into the mid-west and beyond the Mississippi River.

New Yearly Meetings were established. Due, in part, to geographic isolation and the lack of adequate leadership some of the new groups of Friends began to follow divergent practices, sometimes adopting customs and rituals previously not practiced by Friends.

In view of these trends a conference of representatives

from all Yearly Meetings in official correspondence with London Yearly Meeting was called to meet in Richmond, Indiana in October of 1887.

The conference issued the Richmond Declaration of Faith to bring American Friends to a greater unity of purpose and practice.

Following two more conferences held at five-year intervals, in 1902 a formal organization was established to be known as the Five Years Meeting of Friends in America. Twelve Yearly Meetings had previously adopted the Uniform Discipline. They were: New England, New York, Baltimore, Canada, Wilmington (in Ohio), Indiana, Western (in Indiana), Iowa, Kansas, California, Oregon and North Carolina.

Although Kansas and Oregon Yearly Meetings later withdrew over theological differences, new Yearly Meetings have been established and have united in this larger Friends fellowship. They are: Nebraska, Jamaica, Cuba, and East Africa. Friends groups in Mexico and Jordan are also associated with the Friends United Meeting.

Common Testimonies and Distinctive Features

Although the Friends United Meeting includes an amazing variety of Quakers we do have a number of common testimonies.

We believe that God—through His Spirit—can speak directly to anyone, revealing His will. Therefore, in meetings for worship God can use any worshiper as His minister. Some Friends Meetings follow the pattern of "un-programmed" worship; that is, without any pre-arranged order of service. As we silently pray and worship together, God may inspire some worshipers to speak, pray or sing.

Other meetings have felt the need for inspired preaching, pastoral care and skilled teaching. We have made use of Friends pastors possessing gifts in these ministries. The

Friends pastor works to develop the latent gifts for ministry among his fellow-members, and functions as a part of a "team-leadership" rather than dominating the meeting's leadership and ministry. About 80% of the local meetings of the Friends United Meeting in their worship follow an order of service or a semi-programmed meeting with the pastor participating; other meetings follow the pattern of un-programmed worship.

We believe that the experiences of communion with our Lord and the baptism of his Spirit can be known without the use of symbolic ceremonies of these "sacraments."

In all meetings, whether we have a pastor, meeting secretary, or no employed leadership, the monthly meetings for business are a corporate search for Divine ordering of our affairs. All members share an equal responsibility in this search for guidance. Any authority a member may exercise is based on his recognized obedience to the leading of the Holy Spirit, and not by virtue of any position or title held in the meeting's organization.

We believe in the sacredness of personality as a gift of God's creation. Therefore, we support to varying degrees the historic Quaker testimonies for peace (and its corollary not to kill another human being), good race relations, and care for the disadvantaged.

We believe that all of life is to be lived as a stewardship before God. Therefore, we hold to testimonies for integrity in business affairs and speaking the truth without oaths; for personal moral conduct that both respects the sacredness of others and honors the body as a creation of God. Friends discourage the use of narcotics, alcoholic beverages and tobacco.

Any distinctive features of the Friends United Meeting are a matter of emphasis rather than of uniqueness.

We believe in and rely upon the continuing revelation of the Holy Spirit of God who would guide us in our day-today affairs as well as usher us into the Life Eternal. We emphasize the redeeming Grace of God through Jesus Christ our Lord. We believe in the inspiration of the Holy Scriptures. Our statements of faith are based on the life and teaching of Jesus Christ and upon our own experiences of God.

Our ministry encompasses an evangelical concern for the spiritual welfare of our neighbor and a social concern for justice and harmony in the communities of our neighbors.

We also possess a strong concern for mission to others beyond our present fellowship in other parts of the world. Our ministry in mission is evangelical and finds expression through preaching, medical, educational, agricultural and industrial services.

We undertake programs of Christian-Quaker education for our children, youth and adults in Sunday Schools, youth fellowships, camping, seminars, conference and family experiences.

Many local meetings find in singing hymns a satisfying expression of our heart's desire to praise God.

One of the great assets of the Friends United Meeting is the growing spirit of co-operation among its diverse member groups. To an outstanding degree Friends have found within the fellowship of the Friends United Meeting a stimulating balance of such primary Christian emphases as the evangelical, the mystical, the rational and the social. Through working and worshipping together, Friends are experiencing a genuine and practical Christian fellowship that goes beyond theoretical discussions of the virtues of unity.

What Does the Friends United Meeting Do?

The Friends United Meeting has a two-fold task:

1. "Pool" the talents, insights and resources of Friends to extend our Quaker witness throughout the world;

2. Provide practical resources for Yearly, Quarterly and local Meetings as we endeavor to serve our members and communities now in rapid change.

The implementation of this task is given to the following seven program-Boards. Each Board is composed of representatives from the member Yearly Meetings. The activities of the Boards are co-ordinated in a United Services program, which is supported by an annual United Budget. Funds for the United Budget come from Yearly Meetings and individual Friends.

Board on Christian Social Concerns

This Board had its historical origin in 1867 with the formation of the Peace Association of Friends. Its present purpose is to help Friends accept the social responsibilities of their experience in the redemptive and caring love of Christ. It works to help in the establishment of justice and Christian morality among men and peace among nations.

Among its recent activities are Washington Seminars for Quaker leaders, Yearly Meeting Conferences on Moral Responsibility, and a national Friends Conference on Race.

Board on Missions

In 1894 several Yearly Meetings joined in forming the American Friends Board of Foreign Missions. In 1929 the Home Mission Board was merged with this Board.

Its present purpose is to introduce people to that way of life in Christ which can enable them to reach their God-given potential as His sons and daughters. It works to release men from the fears of superstition, the ravages of disease, the darkness of ignorance and the sickness of greed.

In recent years overseas Yearly Meetings have been established and have assumed administrative oversight of what was formerly "mission" work. Today more than fifty American and European personnel are employed by the

Board in Africa, Jamaica and Jordan. In Cuba only monetary assistance to Cuban pastors is now possible. A ministry among Indians of Oklahoma and persons of east Tennessee is also aided by this Board.

Board on Publications

Publication of *The American Friend* began in 1894 when the *Friends Review* (1847) and the *Christian Worker* (1871) were united. Under the editorship of Rufus M. Jones this bi-weekly journal sought to become a unifying influence among scattered Friends groups.

In 1960 *Quaker Life* was launched as successor to *The American Friend.* It is a monthly family magazine containing news, thought-provoking articles, editorials and the liberal use of pictures.

The Board also publishes Sunday School materials edited by the Christian Education Board.

It supervises the Friends Book and Supply House, located in the Central Offices building in Richmond, Indiana. This service agency sells books, Sunday School materials, a wide range of church supplies and equipment to Friends Meetings throughout the world. It also serves many other church groups in the vicinity of Richmond.

The following program Boards have been established since the formation of the Five Years Meeting in 1902.

Board on Evangelism and Church Extension

Although this Board began as one of the original Boards of the Five Years Meeting and was instrumental in establishing two new Yearly Meetings, its continuity of service was broken when it was merged with the American Friends Board of Missions in 1929.

In 1960 the Board was re-established to strengthen and bring into effect new methods of evangelism by Friends. While our population has been increasing, membership among Friends has remained static. This program has stirred Friends to re-vitalize long-established meetings by reviving their spiritual concern for others. It has also been of great assistance to Yearly Meetings in getting new Friends Meetings established both in America and abroad.

In co-operation with the Stewardship Board and the Trustees this Board created the Friends Extension Corporation. This new corporation receives investment monies from individuals, trustee groups and meetings which are loaned to new and existing Friends groups to build meetinghouses.

Board on Christian Education

This Board was formed in 1937 by uniting the Board on Young Friends Activities (1912) and the Board on Religious Education (formerly Board on Bible School Work, 1912). The Board produces or provides the *Penn Curriculum Series* of Sunday Church School materials that include materials from Nursery through Adult age levels.

The Board's work is divided into the following four areas:

1. Children's Work:

   This department prepares and edits pupil and teacher materials for Nursery, Kindergarten, Primary and Junior ages. Laboratory Schools for Childrens Workers are held in the Yearly Meetings to give in-service training to volunteer teachers.

2. Young Friends:

   This department prepares and edits the *Penn Youth Quarterly* and the *Friends* youth magazine. It also provides training opportunities for youth fellowship leaders, camp directors and conference leadership. A popular service for high school students is the Washington and United Nations Seminars on citizenship. It is also providing for a new youth program in East Africa.

3. Adult and Christian Home Life:
This department prepares the *Penn Adult Quarterly* and the *Penn Teacher* for adult classes. It also prepares an annual Family Packet.

4. Leadership Education:
This department provides for teacher-training conferences, supervises the Self-Improvement program for teachers, and provides resource materials for Sunday School superintendents.

Board on Stewardship and Finance

This Board was established in 1960 in order to give aid to local meetings in their year-round stewardship ministry and education programs, Every Member Canvasses, and counselling services to Finance Committees.

It also is responsible for the interpretation and promotion of the United Services program of the Friends United Meeting to secure funds for the United Budget.

In 1965 a Special Gifts program was inaugurated to advise generous Friends in the most effective use of their gifts for our corporate Quaker witness.

Board on Christian Vocations

This Board was formed in 1963 in response to the critical leadership vacuum felt in Friends meetings, colleges and agencies. Its work is to challenge all young Friends to make their vocational choices in response to a Divine Call. It also shares with our most able youth and young adults the great opportunities for ministry and service laid upon Friends.

In co-operation with the Earlham School of Religion this Board is maintaining the distinctive Friends testimony on the ministry.

The Board programs are carried out by a staff of about

30 persons in the Friends Central Offices at 101 Quaker Hill Drive, Richmond, Indiana.

Adjacent to the Central Offices is the Quaker Hill Residence which includes facilities for small conferences, retreats and overnight guests.

The work of these Boards is co-ordinated in the Executive Council of the Friends United Meeting. This body of about 50 Friends leaders, representing both the member Yearly Meetings and the program Boards, meets semi-annually. It conducts the interim business of the Friends United Meeting between its triennial sessions.

Ecumenical Relationships

The Five Years Meeting became a charter member of both the World and National Council of Churches. Before the National Council was formed, membership was maintained in the Federal Council, beginning in the very early history of the Five Years Meeting. Representatives have been regularly appointed to both the General Assembly and the General Board of the National Council of Churches. Friends United Meeting representatives feel that the National Council body welcomes and invites the concerns of Friends. There is no feeling that Friends are considered to be a small or insignificant part of the Council.

Members of the Friends Central Offices staff are active in the four main divisions of the Council. These are: Foreign Missions, Christian Education, Home Missions, and Christian Life and Work. Friends of the Friends United Meeting are active in state and local councils of churches in Ohio, Indiana, Illinois, Iowa, California, North Carolina, Nebraska, Colorado, Minnesota, and others.

• 3 •

FRIENDS GENERAL CONFERENCE
by Lawrence McK. Miller

WHILE FRIENDS GENERAL CONFERENCE as an association of
Yearly Meetings came into being in 1900, its antecedents
were organized during the 19th century and its sense of
identity was determined largely by one of the separations
in American Quakerism early in that century. The first
forerunner was the First-day School General Conference
formed in 1868 by Friends of the "Hicksite" Yearly Meetings who were concerned with the forwarding of the Sunday School movement within these Yearly Meetings. Once
every two years members of these Yearly Meetings gathered
together to compare notes on religious education and to
work together in the production of lesson materials that
could be used by local meetings.

The second forerunner was the Friends Union for Philanthropic Labor, organized in 1881 and bringing together
Friends who had been active in the Underground Railroad
prior to the Civil War and who were working ardently for
peace and for social reform. A later list of departments
and superintendents of philanthropic work reveals the
breadth of concern: child welfare, equal rights, industrial
conditions, narcotics, peace, prison reform, proper publications and amusements, purity, temperance, and work
among colored people. These are the concerns that are today gathered under the heading of "peace and social order" or "peace and service." The Friends Union for Philanthropic Labor was in spirit a forerunner of the Amer-

ican Friends Service Committee as it has developed in recent decades.

Another precursor of Friends General Conference was the Friends Religious Conference, which was formed in 1893 by Friends with a special interest in world religions and which grew in part out of the participation of Friends in the World's Congress of Religions in that same year. The fourth forerunner of Friends General Conference was the Friends Education Conference, established in 1894 to bring together biennially those Friends in the Hicksite Yearly Meetings who had a special concern and responsibility for Friends schools and colleges. These conferences which focussed on different areas of concern frequently met at the same time in the same place, and finally in 1900, in Chautauqua, New York, the four organizations reorganized under the name of "Friends' General Conference." The standing committees of the General Conference largely corresponded to the organizational forerunners.

The seven Yearly Meetings involved both in the antecedent groups and in the formation of Friends General Conference itself were Philadelphia, New York, Genesee (principally Meetings in Canada), Ohio, Illinois, Indiana, and Baltimore. All of these Yearly Meetings had "Orthodox" counterparts, and some had in addition "Conservative" counterparts. For example, there were three Ohio Yearly Meetings until the sessions of Ohio Yearly Meeting (General Conference) were suspended in 1920. All of the other six original Yearly Meetings comprising the General Conference exist in name today, but in three cases they are united Yearly Meetings, the Hicksite Yearly Meetings have joined with their Orthodox and Conservative counterparts to form a new enlarged Yearly Meeting.

The character and thrust of Friends General Conference as an association of Yearly Meetings has been largely determined by the cluster of Quaker beliefs and practices that the Hicksite Yearly Meetings emphasized. It is not the purpose of this chapter to review the issues of the separation in American Quakerism, but it is important in understanding Friends General Conference to realize that the separations resulted in the establishment of Yearly Meetings that were separated from other Yearly Meetings, often within the same geographical area, by differences in doctrinal emphasis and manner of worship and by strong feelings created by the strains of division, not only within local meetings themselves but often within families. For many decades there was little recognition on the part of Friends in one branch of the worth of the convictions and practices of Friends in another branch. It was probably inevitable under these circumstances of mutual hostility that there would be on the part of Friends in one branch misinterpretations and exaggerations of the views and practices of Friends in other branches.

Hicksite Friends were probably distinguished by three general emphases. First, there was the conviction that the authority of the Inner Light or Christ Within was central for Quakers and that it was possible for the same Spirit that was revealed in the Scriptures to be revealed in the lives of contemporary men and women. These Friends contended that God had written on the tablet of the human heart His divine law. Salvation was a constant and repeated spiritual process of renewal. The unit of spiritual value was the individual human spirit. Therefore, these Friends rejected the restrictions of Christocentric orthodoxy while at the same time claiming an allegiance to Jesus Christ.

Secondly, Hicksite Friends had a strong allegiance to the traditional form of Quaker worship, based on expectant waiting for divine guidance. In those areas of the country where the new ideas of pastoral leadership for a meeting and of programmed services were being introduced, Hicksite Friends championed a liberal theological approach along with the conservation of the orthodox manner of worship. In respect to this holding to the traditional form of worship, they were in unity with the Conservative Friends, although they were separated from these Friends in terms of religious thought.

Thirdly, Friends of these Hicksite Yearly Meetings generally held to the view that diversity of approach, both within the Society of Friends and within the Christian family as a whole, was not only to be tolerated but to be encouraged. Local meetings of these Yearly Meetings through the years gradually accepted into their fellowships Friends with differing theological viewpoints, finding their meetings for worship enriched by this diversity and placing an emphasis upon lifelong seeking for religious truth and authentic religious experience. In the opening years of the 20th century, prior to the First World War, this liberal approach found support from some of the dominant Christian theologians of the day.

As with any movement that challenges orthodox and rigid lines of thought, Friends of these Yearly Meetings continually faced the problem of defining the boundaries beyond which a sense of identity would disappear. Some individual Friends and some meetings gradually emphasized the doctrine of the Inner Light to the exclusion of an alive identification with the Christian roots of Quakerism. Other individual Friends and meetings continued to hold to a Christian orientation in life and worship.

All of the General Conference Yearly Meetings in their Books of Discipline up to the present day have recognized Quakerism as Christian both historically and in its present form. For example, Baltimore Yearly Meeting, in its Book of Discipline published in 1962, makes the following introductory statement (in part), following the quotation

of the well-known advice from the Meeting of Elders at
Balby, "for the letter killeth, but the Spirit giveth life":

"The Religious Society of Friends holds as the basis
of its faith the belief that God endows every human
being with a measure of His own Divine Spirit. He
leaves no one without witness, but gives the light of His
truth and presence to men of all classes and races.

"Friends find this manifestation of God in man exem-
plified in Jesus of Nazareth. The Divine Spirit became
so wholly Jesus' own that His teaching, example, and sacrificial life are a full revelation in humanity of the will
of God.

"As within ourselves we become conscious of the same
Spirit (the 'Inner Light' or the 'Christ within'), and as
we submit ourselves to its leadings, we also are enabled
to live in conformity to the will of our Heavenly Father."

The liberal emphases of Friends in the Hicksite Yearly
Meetings and their resistance to movements within the
more orthodox Christian denominations helped to determine the character of Friends General Conference and the
direction of its program. Notably absent were foreign missions. The program of the Conference included no evangelical work as such, but there was a great interest in the
advancement of the Society of Friends, and one of the
most important committees of the Conference throughout
its existence has been the Advancement Committee, at one
time named the Committee for the Advancement of Friends'
Principles. Since the formation of the American Friends
Service Committee in 1917, many individual Friends and
most meetings within the constituent Yearly Meetings of
the Conference have actively supported and participated
in the work of the Committee. So also, have many Friends
and most meetings within the General Conference supported the work of the Friends Committee on National

Legislation, recognizing the AFSC and the FCNL as channels for the expression of Quaker concern and service. Friends General Conference, therefore, has in practice largely restricted its activities to the strengthening of local meetings through visiting, financial assistance, provision of advancement and religious education literature, and conferences.

Up to 1955 the Conference operated with a very small budget and staff. There was only one executive staff member and the budget, exclusive of the biennial conferences themselves, rarely exceeded $25,000 per year. In 1955 three of the constituent Yearly Meetings of the Conference united with their orthodox counterparts, and 9,000 additional Friends thereby came into the Conference. In the ten years since that time the General Conference has initiated new programs, increased its staff, and tripled its budget. In 1959, New England Yearly Meeting, also affiliated with the Friends United Meeting, joined Friends General Conference. In 1960, an independent Quarterly Meeting in Michigan, Green Pastures Quarterly Meeting, joined; and in 1961 South Central Yearly Meeting, composed of local meetings in Texas, Arkansas, Oklahoma, and Louisiana, joined the Conference.

The constitutent Yearly Meetings of the Conference appoint a Central Committee of 155 members, and this Committee meets once a year to give overall direction to Conference program. The Central Committee's Executive Committee, also composed of Friends from all of the constituent Yearly Meetings of the Conference, meets three or four times a year and is the key committee in the General Conference organization. The Executive Committee keeps in close touch with the work of the six standing committees, reviews financial reports submitted by the Treasurer, sets the budget for the Conference, and determines policies within the general mandate of program set by the Central Committee. Friends General Conference has no authority over its member Yearly Meetings. Its once biennial, and now annual, general conferences are not business meetings. They are conferences to which all Friends, from General Conference Meetings and other meetings, are invited. The association of Friends General Conference with an international organization, such as the World Council of Churches, must be approved by all of its constituent Yearly Meetings, since the Conference itself has no authority to act for these Yearly Meetings in respect to such affiliations.

For many Friends, both within General Conference Yearly Meetings and in other Yearly Meetings, Friends General Conference is best known for its biennial gatherings, for many years and today held in Cape May, New Jersey. The "Cape May conference" is a week-long conference for Friends of all ages, with programs for adults, college age young Friends, senior high school young Friends, and children. In recent years close to three thousand Friends have attended these conferences, which combine opportunities to hear outstanding speakers and to meet in discussion groups and round tables on a wide variety of subjects with opportunities for recreation and spiritual refreshment. Through a daily series of lectures attenders are able to hear outstanding Friends in the fields of the Bible, Quakerism, and religious literature. Evening speakers have included both Friends and non-Friends on a full range of topics. While the conferences have frequently had a theme, the broad purpose of the Cape May conferences is to expose a large number of Friends to some of the contemporary expressions of life and thought within the Society of Friends and within the religious world at large and to provide an opportunity for individual participation in the discussion of concerns and problems of interest to Friends.

A separate Junior Conference, involving 700 or 800 children and a staff of nearly 50, provides a unique week of intensive religious education. Parents make their own arrangements for accommodations at the conference and are responsible for their children throughout the afternoons and, in the case of some age groups, also in the evenings. The conference thereby becomes a family experience, and many families over several generations return every two years to this week of education and spiritual search. A Senior High School Section is housed completely separately under the direction of Conference staff, thus enabling the Quaker teen-ager to spend the week with his contemporaries and to benefit from a program especially designed for him.

In 1963 Friends General Conference enlarged its program by having for the first time a General Conference located in the Middle West. Four hundred and fifty Friends attended this first national conference in the Midwest, in Traverse City, Michigan. The daily schedule and the format of the conference were modelled after the Cape May conferences. Half the families attending the conference camped in the nearby State Park, a facility not available in southern New Jersey. There were lectures on Quakerism and on Christian classics. Evening speakers covered the range of Quaker concerns. A similar conference was held in 1965.

The year-round work of Friends General Conference is carried out through six standing committees. The Conference recognizes that the vitality and growth of the Religious Society of Friends is predominantly dependent upon the resources and initiative of the local meeting. While all of the standing committees of the Conference strive to strengthen the local meeting, the Advancement Committee has particularly geared its program to assist the local meeting. One of the most important ways this has been done is to encourage intervisitation between meetings and to make possible visits by staff members. Barnard Walton, who was General Secretary from 1915 to 1951, particularly emphasized the visiting of local meetings. He would visit long enough to become acquainted with individual members of the meeting and to learn something about the spiritual state of the meeting. This personal acquaintance with the members and with the life of the meeting gave him credentials for making suggestions. The number of Monthly Meetings within the constituent Yearly Meetings of the Conference is at the time of this writing 257.

The Advancement Committee has also throughout its existence published leaflets that are useful to local meetings in interpreting the Society of Friends and Quakerism to newcomers. The Committee encourages meetings to reach out in their communities to persons who might be interested in Friends and who might become attenders of the meeting and eventually members. Posters distributed by the Peace and Home Service Committees of London Yearly Meeting are made available to meetings in the United States and Canada. Road signs directing the traveler to a meeting are available. The Committee is interested in the ways by which Friends and their meetings might appropriately publicize and advertise themselves.

In 1955 the Advancement Committee established a Meeting House Fund from which it was possible for Monthly Meetings to obtain grants and loans for the building or purchase of meeting houses. Prior to the establishment of the Meeting House Fund, meetings were dependent entirely upon their own resources, upon the very limited resources of their Yearly Meetings, or upon the generosity of other meetings to which they might appeal. The Meeting House Fund enables individual Friends and meetings to contribute to or invest in a fund which can be drawn upon by those meetings that are growing and need meeting houses or expanded facilities. Mortgage pool notes are sold to investors, and the funds derived from these investments are in turn used for loans. In the first ten years of the Meeting House Fund's existence, grants totalling $50,-000 were given to 32 meetings, and loans totalling $139,000 were made to 25 meetings. Over half of the meetings assisted were in the Middle Western or Far Western regions of the United States. While grants and loans were made to meetings irrespective of affiliation, only meetings within the Conference are solicited for contributions to the Fund.

Of special concern to the Advancement Committee has been the roughly 7,000 non-resident Friends who belong to meetings within the General Conference. Many of these Friends are active in local meetings in spite of maintaining their membership in their "home" meetings, but an even larger number are quite inactive in the Society, sometimes because of being completely geographically removed from a meeting similar to their own. The Advancement Committee has a Fellowship of Non-Resident Friends, members of which receive quarterly mailings of inspirational literature. Conference staff members, when possible, visit members of this Fellowship, helping to keep in touch with the Society.

The Religious Education Committee of Friends General Conference publishes a full line of lesson materials for use in First-day Schools with all age groups. The Committee operates on the premise that First-day Schools should determine their own curriculum, selecting those courses of study that fit their particular needs and situations. Courses of study from other sources are also recommended. The Committee, with the assistance of a staff member, seeks out Friends who will draft lesson material, edits the submitted manuscripts, and then arranges for the course to be tested in one or more meetings. The Committee publishes a catalogue of lesson and resource materials available from Friends General Conference written by and for Friends.

The Committee keeps in direct touch with First-day School teachers by issuing and sending to them without charge a quarterly Religious Education *Bulletin.* This *Bulletin* keeps the teacher informed of newly published materials, summarizes results of religious education seminars and workshops, and serves as a means of communication among teachers in this field. Once a year the Committee sponsors the "Rufus Jones Lecture," designed to bring to the Society of Friends leaders in the religious education field, both Friends and non-Friends. The lecture is always followed by a week end seminar, giving members of the Religious Education Committee an opportunity to discuss the lecture with the lecturer himself. As in the case of all standing committees of the Conference, the Religious Education Committee works closely with comparable committees at the Yearly Meeting level.

In 1963, the Central Committee of Friends General Conference established the Religious Life Committee, in order to emphasize and bring into focus the services of the Conference that are particularly directed to the strengthening of the meeting for worship. The Religious Life Committee inherited one of the Conference's most dynamic programs, the Quaker Dialogue Program, under the leadership of Rachel Davis DuBois of New York Yearly Meeting. The purpose of the Dialogue Program is to stimulate at the local meeting level, through skilled leadership, the communication of members with one another and thereby to enable the meeting as a whole to achieve a deeper spiritual level. Since 1958, when the Quaker Dialogue Program began, there have been Dialogues in close to 300 meetings across the United States and in Canada. Workshops have trained other leaders who are skilled in the techniques of group conversation, the basic tool in the Dialogues.

The Religious Life Committee in the brief time of its existence has sponsored a conference at Pendle Hill on the vocal ministry, has worked closely with the Committees on Ministry and Counsel or Meetings on Worship and Ministry of constituent Yearly Meetings, and has engaged in some research on the conditions most favorable to vital meetings for worship.

A fourth standing committee of the Conference is the Education Committee, expressing the concern of the association for Friends schools and colleges. The Committee appoints representatives to the Friends Council on Education, a national body of Friends providing services to Quaker schools and colleges and serving as something of a clearing house. The Conference makes a regular annual appropriation to the Friends Council on Education.

Recognizing that many individual Friends within the meetings of the General Conference are active in the American Friends Service Committee and Friends Committee on National Legislation and in Yearly Meeting committees on peace and social order, Friends General Conference maintains a relatively modest program in the field of peace and social concerns through its Peace and Social Order Committee. The Committee has been responsive to invitations to Friends General Conference to have representatives at various Quaker and non-Quaker national gatherings on concerns in the peace and social order field. The Committee cooperates with other Quaker organizations in the sponsorship of special gatherings, such as the Vigil at the Pentagon in Washington, D.C. in 1960, and the Friends Witness for World Order in 1962. The Committee has sponsored with Young Friends of North America a summer peace caravan.

Foremost among the activities of the Peace and Social Order Committee over the years has been the representation of Friends General Conference as a Non-Governmental Organization at the United Nations. Thousands of Friends through this program have been introduced to the United Nations, either on one-day study tours or at two-day conferences. The Conference's Accredited Representative has reported back to Friends on the activities of the international organization, either through the pages of the *Friends Journal* or directly to committees and meetings of the Conference. In 1965 the direct accreditation of the Conference as a Non-Governmental Organization at the United Nations was terminated in favor of all Quaker organizations being recognized by the UN through the Friends World Committee for Consultation. However, the Conference's work at the United Nations continues, as before, in close cooperation with the Quaker Program at the United Nations of the AFSC and the FWCC.

The sixth standing committee of the Conference is the Committee on Christian Unity, which is concerned with the ecumenical relationships of Friends General Conference. Friends General Conference is a member of the World Council of Churches, having joined the Council at the time it was formed in 1948. The Conference has expressed its hesitations regarding the creedal form of the basis of membership of the World Council of Churches but has not been successful in having the basis of membership changed more nearly in accord with Quaker preferences. The General Conference has felt that the opportunity to participate in the deliberations and activities of the World Council, and the contribution other churches can make to the Society of Friends through the channel of the World Council, outweigh the disadvantages of belonging to an organization with which there is substantial disagreement at some points. The General Conference has stated its reservations regarding the basis of membership on two occasions. The World

Council through its Secretariat recognizes these reservations, but has encouraged Friends to continue their participation in the ecumenical organization.

Friends General Conference has also had a long-standing, but somewhat uncertain, relationship to the International Association for Liberal Christianity and Religious Freedom, a predominantly Unitarian body. Not all Yearly Meetings of Friends General Conference have agreed that the Conference should apply for membership. Similarly, there is not unanimity in the constituent Yearly Meetings regarding the Conference applying for membership in the National Council of Churches.

The Committee on Christian Unity coordinates the participation of representatives from Friends General Conference at the various ecumenical gatherings sponsored by the World Council of Churches and in some cases by other ecumenical bodies. The Committee has been particularly interested to assist Young Friends in their ecumenical contacts. In 1964, the Committee co-sponsored a gathering of Friends, Mennonites, and Brethren, a consultation designed to bring members of these churches into closer fellowship.

In terms of program, staff and budget, Friends General Conference has undoubtedly reached a plateau, since the ten years beginning in 1955 resulted in expansion that strained the financial resources available to the Conference. The Conference is dependent upon appropriations from its constituent Yearly Meetings and contributions from concerned individual Friends and Monthly Meetings. It is likely that in the near future the Conference will carefully evaluate its program in the light of the social crises in the United States and of the increasing interest in Friends on the part of students. Many of the meetings that the Conference services are college and university meetings that have grown up because of the interest of young adults and families in Quaker testimonies and projects and which are now searching for a basis of ministry to the academic community. The social crises include the rapid technological developments that result in automation, the revolution in sex morality, the loss of privacy resulting from growth in population and the urbanization of the United States, the dominance of public decisions in the lives of individuals, and the concentration on materialistic values in American culture.

At its conferences and through the work of its standing committees the Conference hopes to be able to take some initiative and provide some leadership to local meetings as they and their members face these crises in our times. The services of the Conference will hopefully be adjusted to meet new needs and conditions. The Conference is committed to working with other groups of Friends where such cooperation is mutually beneficial. The Conference endeavors to be sensitive to the following advice from the *Faith and Practice* of Philadelphia Yearly Meeting:

. . . Friends are advised to keep in mind that right actions arise only from the right Source within. Activities which come out of a spirit of business or of self-importance or which serve only to enhance the record of a committee or an organization are deadening and should be distinguished from deeds inspired by God's Spirit of Love and Truth working in the heart.

• 4 •

EVANGELICAL FRIENDS ALLIANCE

by Arthur O. Roberts

DURING THE YEARLY MEETING SESSIONS of 1965, Ohio, Kansas, Oregon, and Rocky Mountain gave final consideration and approval of the Evangelical Friends Alliance, an organization designed to unite for action in specified areas, and already drawing together in closer fellowship the independent, evangelical yearly meetings of America.

In addition to organizational procedures already in partial operation, the recommendations acted upon include a statement of faith embodying in brief form principles adhered to by these yearly meetings. A summary will help identify the evangelical position.

The statement of faith acclaims the Bible as the inspired rule of faith, subject to the Holy Spirit as true interpreter. Clearly expressed are the sovereignty of God, the vicarious atonement offered in Jesus Christ through His death and resurrection, the work of the Holy Spirit experientially with men to bring them to salvation. Man is shown as sinful but redeemable; salvation is stated to comprise both forgiveness and sanctification. The church is acknowledged as the visible expression of Christ and its fulfillment in the final resurrection and judgment affirmed. The "spiritual realities" of inward and corporate communion and the baptism with the Holy Spirit are stressed, and the Christian witness through word and deed elaborated in terms of general and particular ministry. One section offers Christian love where-

58

in unessential differences may be accepted. But no effort is made to handle any of the moral or ethical advices or queries dealt with by the yearly meeting disciplines.[1]

In addition to the statement of faith, the recommendations include formation of a commission of moral action. The other commissions include missions, church extension, publications, youth, and Christian education.

In general the commissions seek to utilize common literature, procedures, programs, and promotion in the respective areas of concern.

Who are These Evangelical Friends?

Who are the people in these yearly meetings who have banded together for mutual action, and what distinguishes them from other Friends? In combination they comprise approximately 30,000 Friends, including those younger churches in countries to which missionaries have gone. These Friends are conservative in theology. They stress the reality of experiencing Jesus Christ as personal Saviour and Lord. They hold to the importance of the Bible and trust it as the outward word of God, whose inward Word, Christ, has been confirmed to them in spiritual experience. They would generally acknowledge the Richmond Declaration of Faith as a fair statement of their Christian beliefs.

The individual meetings make use of local pastors whose gifts are recognized by the yearly meeting. Sunday morning worship embodies singing, Scripture reading, a period of open worship—usually—and a sermon by the pastor. Evening meetings are frequently more open to testimony, exhortation and prayer, and to evangelistic appeal.

In the usual assortment of committees, local, quarterly meeting, and yearly meeting, concerns find expression. Most churches engage in some form of special public evangelistic

---

[1] See end of chapter for bibliographical references.

meetings annually as well as encouraging direct spiritual witnessing on the part of their members. They are committed to church extension, seeking not only the conversion of those about them, but also those in other lands.

Their ecumenical relationships among Friends may be limited by geography or doctrines. Many share Everett Cattell's "passion for unity" on the basis of theological consensus rather than on the basis of heritage or name.[2] Among other groups these Friends participate in bodies such as the National Association of Evangelicals (rather than the National Council of Churches), the National Holiness Association, Youth For Christ, the Billy Graham evangelistic crusades, World Vision, and, on campuses, Inter-varsity Christian Fellowship.

Pastors and other leading Friends would subscribe to *Christianity Today* rather than to *Christian Century*. Many are active in the Association of Evangelical Friends. Several participate in the Quaker Theological Discussion Group.

Of the four yearly meetings, Ohio is the oldest. Established in 1813, Ohio suffered two severe splits during its first century: the Hicksite split and the Wilbur-Gurney separation. Headquarters are at Damascas, Ohio.

The Wesleyan aspect of the post Civil War revival, which so signally awakened mid-western Quakers, stamped its image heavily upon Ohio Friends. They found Christian fellowship in the camp meetings, the National Holiness Association, and the Bible School movement. Cleveland Bible School, under the leadership of Walter Malone and others, trained Friends leaders influential in many areas of Quakerdom. Established first in Cleveland early in the century, the college removed to Canton, Ohio, in 1957, becoming known as Malone College. Everett Cattell, widely-respected Friends missionary statesman and president of the World Evangelical Alliance, is the current president of Malone.

Ohio's mission fields include India and Formosa. The work there was formerly in mainland China. One of their missionaries, W. E. DeVoll, is head of the Medical Center of the United Mission to Nepal. This missionary assignment to a country only recently opened to the Christian witness has been accepted as a joint project by the Alliance. In 1965 the first conscientious objector, a young Friend from Oregon, went there to serve as a medical technologist.

In India the Bundelkhand Christian Friends' Society, largely indigenous, reflects Ohio's missionary vision for that country. Part of Ohio's efforts in India include ecumenical cooperation in the Union Theological Seminary of Yeotmal and the work of individuals in various evangelical fellowships. Clifton Robinson, for example, was associate secretary general for Asia, of the International Council for Christian Leadership. He has been used on occasion for leadership among the Mar Thoma Church of Kerala, thus helping bridge a gap between Christian missions and the older indigenous Christian groups.

Kansas Yearly Meeting was established in 1872 in the westward migrations. A great rural yearly meeting, it has provided many persons for widespread Quaker leadership. During the years of the dust storms and shrinking farm populations it sent its families farther to the west, to California and Oregon. In recent years it has accepted the challenge for new city churches and has erected a number of fine new meetinghouses in major cities of Kansas, Oklahoma, Texas, and Missouri. There are about 8500 members. Friends University in Wichita, and Friends Academy and Bible College at Haviland, are its schools. Outstanding among the many missionaries coming from Kansas was the Arthur Chilson family. Arthur Chilson helped in the development of the pioneer industrial mission in Kenya, out of which came East Africa Yearly Meeting. In 1937 Kansas founded its own mission field in the country of Burundi.

This work has weathered the severe storms marking the transition of central Africa from colonial to independent status. An excellent feature of the mission work is the Central Africa Broadcasting Company, known as Radio CORDAC.

Begun Christmas Day, 1964, the station broadcasts in four major languages: Kirundi (understood by about 6 million people within its range), Kiswahili, a trade language used by millions, French, and English—second languages for Congolese and East African people. Hopes are for a 50,000 watt transmitter whereby the station can reach 180,-000,000 people for the Gospel ministry. James E. Morris and Robert Kellum direct the staff of this station.

Oregon Yearly Meeting resulted largely from the migrations of Iowa and Kansas Friends. It was set up by the former in 1893. 6000 members in the three Pacific Northwest states of Oregon, Washington, and Idaho comprise its membership. In certain ways the character of Friends here is marked by the last pioneering ventures in the West. Numbers of Friends settled in colonies gathered on land newly-opened to agriculture by irrigation projects. The writer's father settled in a tar-paper shack on a new eighty acre tract, clearing the sagebrush to plant grain and alfalfa. Churches followed these land developments—and still do, while in the Pacific coast cities the meetings develop in the suburbs. Half of the sixty-four meetings have been established since 1930.

Friends Academy in the farm community of Greenleaf, Idaho, arose under the care of pioneer Quaker families in the Boise valley, in the first decade of the century and continues to serve the families as a secondary day school. George Fox College, formerly Pacific College, began at Newberg, Oregon, as a grammar and secondary school in 1885. Herbert Hoover was one of the most illustrious of its first students. The College, established in 1891 is a vigorous liberal arts school. Of its 350-400 students more than half are Friends, drawn largely from the Northwest and California. Milo Ross, well-known Quaker minister, has served as president since 1954.

Oregon has a significant youth program, including summer camping at several conference grounds, and a youth ambassador program for summer service to meetings.

Oregon's mission program reaches into Bolivia and Peru, on behalf of the oppressed, ancient people, the Aymara, who inhabit the altiplano of the two countries. Pressured by various revolutions and land reforms, the thirty-year old missionary work has shifted dramatically to an indigenous program. The initials INELA stand for the National Friends Church of Bolivia, self-governed and self-supporting in its local and yearly meeting affairs. Oregon adopted a "hands off" policy until asked in to assist in education, evangelism, and publication. A people barely literate, they are zealous for the Lord Jesus Christ and propagate the Gospel in their own, effective way. The 3000 Friends believers have a firm Christian base. Although the work has been acclaimed a model Christian witness by students of Latin America, Oregon Friends know the price paid in loss of financial investment, stoning of missionaries, and anxieties attendant upon yielding leadership to seemingly poorly-prepared nationals.

The thrust of new outreach among the Aymara is now along the Peruvian shores of Lake Titicaca.

Rocky Moutain Yearly Meeting was set off by Nebraska in 1957, when it appeared most meetings preferred independence to membership in the National Council of Churches via the Five Years Meeting. Since that time the 1500 members have established a mission among the Navajo Indians of Arizona, not greatly distant from their own churches in the west and southwest, with a boarding school at Rough Rock. The missionaries move among the scattered tribal peoples, evangelizing from hogan to hogan.

Rocky Moutain has a small membership scattered over a wide area. They profit from the Alliance almost more

than any of the other yearly meetings. Being somewhat
centrally located, they have served as hosts to several of
its planning conferences.

Historic Context

These four yearly meetings ought not to be considered in
isolation from other American yearly meetings. The bonds
of fellowship reach beyond the particular Alliance through
which they have chosen to find certain areas of cooperation.
Intermingling takes place between the independent, evangelical yearly meetings and their counterparts in the Five
Years Meeting. Pastors shift from one yearly meeting to
another, and families moving to new areas quickly identify
across these boundaries. The pattern of Quietism was broken
for these four as it was for members of the Five Years Meeting (now called Friends United Meeting). The revivals in
Indiana and Iowa in the post-Civil war years swept across
the American yearly meetings with creative results, building upon the evangelical emphasis given earlier by Gurney.

Upon reading the documents of the uniting conferences
of the last decade of the nineteenth century, one is struck
by the fact that Edmund Stanley of Kansas, or John Henry
Douglas of Oregon, or J. Walter Malone, of Ohio, mingle
in evangelical fellowship and hope with men from Wilmington, or Baltimore, or New York, or London.

But within two decades the visions of unity shattered on
the rocks of the modernist-fundamentalist rift which en-
gulfed American Protestant Christianity. Ohio, like Philadelphia, but for different reasons, had not accepted the
Richmond Declaration of Faith nor joined the Five Years
Meeting. Ohio came later to espouse the position of David
Updegraff on the Sacraments or ordinances: allowing "lib-
erty of conscience" on the matter (he opposed making "non-
essentials" into articles of faith).[3]

Indeed, in the cooperative endeavor of the Alliance, the

yearly meetings have sought to be sensitive to Ohio's permissiveness without denying their own traditional Quaker position.

Oregon withdrew from the Five Years Meeting in 1926, Kansas in 1937, and Rocky Mountain (essentially) when it was set up as independent by Nebraska in 1957. The issues of theological liberalism were involved in each case. Oregon and Kansas Friends felt especially grieved by liberal-conservative contradictories which appeared in mission and publication personnel and activities. They felt the Christian message was being clouded by unbelief and the dilution of the Gospel. They were and have continued often to be grieved at the substitution of humanistic service for evangelistic activity. They have resisted efforts to diminish the place and inspiration of the Scriptures and the Quaker emphasis on holiness. Placed on the defensive in earlier years they have sometimes hedged their opposition with lesser issues or reactionary positions, but they have attempted to hold up what they conceived was a true Biblical and Quaker position.

Although fellowship with yearly meetings within the Five Years Meeting remained real in many ways, contacts became fewer, and regionalism was often the price paid for a conservative stand. Participation in the camp meeting movement, Bible School work, and sacrificial missionary service tended to compensate for the larger fellowship from which they withdrew. But they yearned for greater Quaker unity.

Movements of Renewal

The Evangelical Friends Alliance represents *one* corporate step of denominational unity, brought about as a result of several movements of spiritual renewal within the Society of Friends. These movements are: 1) the general evangelical renewal within Christianity, 2) the new scholarly recognition of the evangelical nature of seventeenth century Quakerism, and 3) the Association of Evangelical Friends.

The effect of the first has been to drive Quakers out of a non-theological middle ("muddle"!) toward either a Christ-centered Quakerism or a humanistic one. The climate of evangelical theology has enabled Friends once characterized as "fundamentalists" to find a context of vigorous Christian support in conservative theology.

A major, if quiet, Quaker revolution in the mid-twentieth century has been the scholarly recovery of the evangelical perspectives of our early Quaker heritage. The labors of Canby Jones, Wilmer Cooper, Hugh Barbour, Maurice Creasey, Lewis Benson, the present writer, and others attest to current recognition of the essentially Christ-centered nature of normative Quakerism. The effects of this revolution are latent among our youth who are prone to ask of their heritage, "Can these bones live?"

The Association of Evangelical Friends is a loosely-knit movement of rather casual, individual membership. The main thrust has come from a series of triennial conferences, the seventh of which met July 28–August 1, 1965, at Haviland, Kansas, and from the quarterly, *Concern,* begun in 1959. An effort to establish a summer seminar proved unworkable and was abandoned.

The conferences have met regularly since 1947, drawing Friends from within and outside the Five Years Meeting, but with the greatest participation from the evangelicals. These have been times of spiritual renewal for the hundreds who have assembled, meeting at various places from West to East. The Association resisted all efforts to involve it in corporate actions, such as launching a mission field or acting for official Quakerdom. As Gerald Dillon, president, has pointed out, the call for revival has come from many quarters and many individuals, whether connected with the Association or not, for Friends "are thirsting to see again the spiritual fervency within Quakerdom that characterized the first decade of our church itself."[4]

The journal *Concern* has articulated the nature of this yearning for renewal with articles varying from historical sketches of early Quaker practice to contemporary evaluations of current Christian and Quaker movements. Especially evocative were Everett Cattell's "Passion for Unity," Charles Beals' "Historical Roots of Evangelical Friends," Canby Jones' "The Lamb's War," and the editor's "Evangelical Unity Among Friends" and "Friends and the Holiness Movement."[5]

The Association of Evangelical Friends at its meeting in 1965 approved the calling of a conference on "Doctrine," in July, 1966, at Rockcleft Camp, near Colorado Springs, Colorado. Some 40 Friends will be invited to the conference which the Association hopes will bring Biblical insights to bear upon a number of theological issues. "The nature of the church," "The meaning of authority," and "Christian Holiness," are three issues which will be considered as Friends seek the leading of the Holy Spirit and the help of scripture. They hope to reach an understanding of normative Quaker views, and the modifications of these positions which have occurred over the past three hundred years. Participation will be by invitation, and will include widely representative Friends from across America.

The Association has served as a catalyst for renewal both within the Five Years Meeting, and among evangelical yearly meetings. On the other hand, the Evangelical Friends Alliance gathered Friends concerned for united efforts, and then the yearly meetings took up the responsibility for translating vision into action.

In 1963 a missions conference was gathered by the Association. A number of American yearly meetings responded. The *Missionary Voice*, a missionary magazine serves as an

information-inspiration piece for the seven mission fields of
the four yearly meetings.

The youth of the several yearly meetings have combined
their efforts in several ways. They are no longer called
"Christian Endeavor," but "Friends Youth," with sweat
shirts emblazoned with the emblem! They even have a new
magazine, *Accent.* During the summer of 1965 one hundred ten selected high school youth met at a Friends Youth
Leadership Conference under the newly-formed Youth Commission of the Alliance. Youth, as always, have cut through
formalities faster than their elders, and their cooperative
ventures have given them a vision of the Friends Church
which comprises a significant feature of the Alliance.

Common procedures in considering missionary candi-
dates should help Quakers answer God's call to service
within the framework of some Quaker opportunity. Plans
call, too, for a joint publication supplanting the present
yearly meeting papers, avoiding duplication of effort and
expense, and providing a more attractive magazine and
wider coverage of important articles.

Relationship to Other Friends

How does the Alliance relate to other Friends? Will it
be divisive? It should be understood that the move is
toward unity from hitherto separate groups. The stated purpose reads: "The Evangelical Friends Alliance shall serve
as the united voice and work for the mutual benefit of the
member yearly meetings, to pursue cooperatively the work
of the Lord and to strengthen the work of the Friends
church."[6]

Friends have been tender toward problems relating to
the Friends United Meeting. There is no desire to gather
in dissident monthly or quarterly meetings. Under pressure
from liberalism from time to time some Friends have felt
the same sort of strain which prompted the movements of
separation earlier. But the Alliance proposed membership

by yearly meeting only, thus recognizing the unit of authority among Friends.[7]

Quite generally leaders within the Friends United Meeting look upon the Alliance as a meaningful relationship among the evangelicals and a complement of their own renewals.

Commenting upon the January, 1965 conference which drew up the final recommendations for the Constitution, Dean Gregory, elected president, stated: "The conference was marked by a great degree of hope and optimism for a closer unity among Friends and a greater vision for the task of the church—to adequately interpret by word and deed the central message of the Gospel of Christ in the world. . . . Friends moved prayerfully and carefully to a new level of understanding, vision, cooperation and action."[8]

The Alliance is not the Friends Church, but it is a step of faith on the part of four yearly meetings who look toward a Friends Church, world-wide in scope and evangelical in nature. It strengthens present bonds of fellowship and gathers that which was scattered, looking to Christ to lead us back to wholeness.

References

[1]Minutes of the Evangelical Friends Alliance, January, 1965. Mimeographed copy.

[2]*Concern,* journal of the Association of Evangelical Friends (Newberg, Oregon: Barclay Press), I, 3, Fall, 1959.

[3]For a recent presentation of Updegraff's position see *Concern,* VII, 2, Spring, 1965.

[4]*Concern,* II, 4, Fall, 1960.

[5]See, respectively, Vols. I, 3; II, 1; II, 4; III, 3; and V, 3. Readers will find helpful contemporary analyses in various issues of the *Quaker Religious Thought.*

[6]Evangelical Friends Alliance minutes, January, 1965. Mimeographed copy.

[7]*Ibid.,* see Article V.

[8]*Concern,* VII, 1, Winter, 1965.

• 5 •

CONSERVATIVE FRIENDS
by William P. Taber, Jr.

A VISITOR AMONG CONSERVATIVE FRIENDS* about thirty years ago might justly have regarded their way of life as a "museum Quakerism" which, while steadily declining and decaying, preserved some of the forms and spirit of early nineteenth-century Quakerism. The same visitor returning today will find that most of Conservative Quakerism has left its museum-like isolation and has rejoined the world Society of Friends (as individual Conservatives have been doing for fifty years). At first, our visitor's former conviction that Conservatives must continually decline in numbers, as they have during most of their history, would seem to be verified, for three of the six Conservative yearly meetings in 1935 have gone out of existence, and the remaining three are smaller than they were then. However, the remaining yearly meetings have begun to show signs of new growth as they have been joined by at least six new urban or college meetings. The visitor will also find that many of the customs which survived thirty years ago are nearly gone today; for example, the plain Quaker clothing is rare in almost all meetings, and the plain language is heard much less frequently today. Here and there he will

---

* I have used the word *Conservative* throughout this essay only because it is the most commonly used term. It may be helpful to bear in mind that Conservative Friends may, in many cases, be liberal or even radical on political, social, or peace issues, and that they cannot be described, as a body, as being theologically conservative. *Wilburite* might be a less misleading term.

even find a new meetinghouse without the traditional facing bench, and with the chairs or benches all facing each
other; and in most of the old meetinghouses he will find
that it no longer matters whether he sits on the men's or
women's side of the aisle unless he is asked to sit on the
facing bench. Finally he will discover many changes in
the procedure and spirit of the business meeting; in only
one monthly meeting will he find separate men's and wom-
en's business meetings, and in most meetings he will find
an eager interest in sharing the local, national, and international concerns of Friends.

In spite of these sweeping changes, Conservative Quakerism still has a distinct flavor which can be traced to its
roots in the nineteenth century when John Wilbur's blunt
warnings about the outcome of the evangelical doctrines
led to the disownments and separations of the Conservatives. However tolerantly modern Conservatives may feel
about the evolution taken by most of Quakerism after 1845,
their ancestors who lived through the Wilburite separations
from 1845 to 1902 felt that Wilbur's prophecies had come
true with the rise of the pastoral system, and the use of
music in many American meetings. Disowned and isolated
from the rest of Quakerism (with the exception of Philadelphia) the Conservatives drew together in colonies and
zealously maintained the culture they had inherited. Eventually the Conservative yearly meetings set up correspondence among their various colonies in New England, North
Carolina, Ohio, Indiana, Canada, Iowa, and Kansas. (Later
they corresponded with the group centered at Fritchley,
England.)

Although they were steadily declining in numbers, they
enjoyed a kind of golden age in the last two decades of
the nineteenth century, when the revolutions in agriculture
and communication were still far enough in the future for
these largely agricultural and small-town colonies to per-

fect and protect a Quakerism which thought of itself as avoiding the extremes of Hicksism and Gurneyism, and which believed it had preserved both the form and the spirit of ancient Quakerism. The way of life which developed was a conscious attempt to preserve and cultivate sensitivity to the inner leadings so that each person's life, in all details, was governed by the Spirit. Paradoxically, the memory of two disastrous separations led to a legalism and a rigidity (about certain Quaker forms) which no doubt contributed to continual loss of membership until Conservative leaders in this century developed more of an understanding of history and psychology.

The early Conservatives sought to guard the education of their children in their own (usually rural) schools and in several boarding schools under their strict control. Their numbers were large enough to offer a great many choices to young people seeking a marriage partner, a congenial community, and an occupation. In spite of the distance between the scattered colonies, they were in frequent contact through visits to relatives and friends (they became somewhat intermarried) and through the frequent travels of their ministers, who sought to be scrupulously obedient to the slightest call of the Spirit within them. Some of their ministers, who were untouched by higher education, evidently combined great talents with a keen sensitivity to the psychic world. Thus, secure in the belief that they were the last remnant of the great people which Fox had gathered, and that they were being led by able men and women, Conservative Friends remained in partial isolation from the world and from other Friends for a number of years.

Since 1900 the old serene semi-isolation from the world has become increasingly impossible, as changing methods in farming and business, rising standards of education (and the mobility of the educated), two World Wars, declining membership, and developments in world Quakerism have all contributed to bringing the Conservatives back into the mainstream of Quaker life. For a time it looked as if these groups would be unable to halt their steady loss of members, which was accentuated by the laying down of Kansas Yearly Meeting in 1929 and Western (in Indiana) in 1962. Another apparent sign of eventual decay of a way of life was the closing down of almost all Conservative schools by the time of the Second World War; only one boarding school, Barnesville, and about two elementary schools remained. (Several schools have opened since the war). The increasing numbers of college-trained Conservatives usually found employment in cities and colleges far from any Conservative meeting. Some of these became active in the new university and city meetings or in the old urban meetings, while others gladly entered into other denominations to escape what they regarded as a narrow Quakerism concerned only about petty details. Some of these, who had a strong instinct toward the ministry, became pastors. A few of the young people who had shared in Quaker service and Quaker concerns since the First World War may have left the Conservatives to join with Friends less afraid of "creaturely activity." Another factor which indicated—and may have contributed to—decline was the weakening of the discipline, which remained almost unchanged, but was no longer enforced in the old way. In spite of what the discipline said, almost no one under middle age wore plain clothing by 1940, many families had music in their homes, people were not disowned for "marrying out," and growing numbers of nominal members who never attended meeting were allowed to remain on the rolls without any attempt to reclaim or release them.

In the years since 1940 many forces have led to a renewal of Conservative vitality, even though most of the rural meetings have continued to lose members. The great challenges of the Second World War and the years that have followed led all Conservative Yearly Meetings into active cooperation with other Friends in support of the AFSC and other agencies which aided the conscientious objector and worked for peace. As the peace testimony had always been strongly supported in Conservative groups, a majority of their active members of military age were conscientious objectors during the war and under the conscription laws which have followed it. They provided financial support and some leadership for the CPS camps. A few young men were sent to prison during the war, and a larger number went to prison during the following five years. A majority of active members still choose alternative service when they are conscripted. Like their fathers or cousins who were sent to camps and hospitals all over the United States during the last war, these young people —especially those who have served abroad—bring back much vitality to their home meetings when they return. The Peace Committees of the surviving yearly meetings have been active ever since the beginning of the war, or even earlier, and they have continued to keep open the channels to wider Quakerism and the wider peace movement. Iowa Friends cooperated in maintaining a refugee hostel at Scattergood, near West Branch. In some cases Peace Committees have provided funds for up-to-date peace literature for their own and other schools, as well as speakers for meetings, schools, and neighboring communities. They have regularly broadened their horizons by encouraging (and aiding financially) their members and their boarding school students to visit legislators in Washington and other places. They sent substantial delegations to the two large Quaker Peace Witnesses in Washington, and a few of their members have taken part in some of the radical peace action projects. At least one yearly meeting (Ohio) holds an annual Peace Workshop in an effort to get at the roots of pacifist integrity and effective pacifist action.

Most Conservatives would probably agree with those Quakers who say that the peace testimony, to be effective, must arise out of a life which has been transformed and made consistent by the power of the Light within. Although they have learned to be increasingly articulate and analytical about their reasons for pacifism, many of them still rest their argument on the words and example of Christ and on the inner Witness. Although they generally support peace education and pressure for governmental moves toward peace, they also stress the importance of each individual's developing the psychological and spiritual qualities of which pacifism is a by-product, and of the great importance of each person's obedience to his specific leadings.

Since the war the Conservative Yearly Meetings have resumed correspondence with all other yearly meetings, though they frequently send special epistles to each other, the group in Costa Rica, and the remnant in Indiana. They have embraced most national and international agencies of Friends, in most cases providing some financial support and appointing representatives. Cooperation with other Friends went so far in two Conservative Yearly Meetings that they merged with other groups—New England in 1945, and Canada in 1955. The former Conservatives in both unions appear to be taking their full share of leadership, finding new life and fulfillment in their enlarged Quaker sphere.

The Conservative world of today includes three yearly meetings, still primarily rural—though many members engage in non-agricultural occupations—and several outposts. A small remnant of Western Yearly Meeting (Indiana) exists as an independent meeting at Plainfield. A small meeting at Fairhope, Alabama, belongs to Ohio Yearly Meeting, and a small one in Pasadena, California, belongs to Iowa. A remnant of Kansas Yearly Meeting at Galena, Kansas, also belongs to Iowa. About half of Fairhope meeting, in a desire to escape American militarism and materialism, migrated to Costa Rica in 1950, where they set up an agricultural colony and established Monte Verde Meeting, which is now independent, though its members still maintain ties with friends and relatives in the Conservative Yearly Meetings. A recent unofficial tabulation lists the total membership of these groups at just under 2,000. Between them they operate four day schools, two boarding schools, and a home for elderly Friends (Barnesville).

Each of the three remaining yearly meetings has developed a growing interest in cooperation and intervisitation with neighboring Friends. In North Carolina this has taken the form of cooperation in some projects with the FUM Yearly Meeting which controls Guilford College, and it has led to special concern for the new independent meetings springing up in their area. One of these new meetings, at Durham, has joined the Conservative Yearly Meeting. North Carolina Conservatives gained another new meeting when some of their members founded the meeting at Virginia Beach, Virginia. Another new meeting is being started experimentally near Murfreesboro, North Carolina.

In Iowa the situation is somewhat similar; there is some cooperation with the FUM Yearly Meeting—which also controls a college—in local Service Committee work and some other affairs. Two local meetings share or cooperate with FUM meetings in Sunday school programs. Since 1950, the Iowa Conservative Yearly Meeting has been joined by four urban or college meetings, which now make up more than one seventh of the active membership of the yearly meeting. As in North Carolina, some of the members of these new meetings came from Conservative backgrounds, but the majority represent a gain of new members and new life in the yearly meeting. Recently Iowa Conservatives have held a mid-year meeting to which members of the Missouri Valley Association of new meetings were invited. On at least one occasion the Missouri Valley Association met concurrently with the mid-year meeting.

Ohio's movement for intervisitation and cooperation is complicated by the fact that six yearly meetings overlap in Ohio; these are Indiana (FUM), Indiana (FGC), Wilmington (FUM), Ohio (Evangelical), Ohio (C), and Lake Erie Yearly Meeting and Association. For many years some Ohio Conservatives have been concerned to visit the new meetings which are now in the Lake Erie Yearly Meeting and Lake Erie Association, and Conservative Friends have occasionally joined these meetings, even holding dual membership and being active in both groups. Some Conservative meetings and some nearby Lake Erie Yearly Meeting/ Association meetings join in a program of monthly intervisitation, and the Conservative Yearly Meeting cooperates with Indiana (FGC), Lake Erie and Wilmington (FUM) in a Continuing Committee on Greater Unity which has sponsored two summer conferences to bring Friends in the Ohio-Lake Erie Yearly Meeting area closer together. Twice in recent years the Lake Erie Association has met concurrently with Ohio Yearly Meeting at Barnesville. A new step toward understanding was taken recently when a few representatives of Ohio (Evangelical) and Ohio (C) met together to discuss evangelism; this was probably the first official contact between these geographically overlapping yearly meetings since their separation in 1854 and the subsequent legal contest.

A distinctive feature of all of the surviving Conservative yearly meetings is their interest in children and young people, which has sometimes made the Conservative subculture seem like one great inter-related family (which is partly true). Perhaps dwindling numbers and the rural orientation of most Conservative Friends may be partly responsible for their interest in youth and for their valuing the opinions and service of the young. Some yearly meet-

ings and local meetings regularly appoint young people—
including an occasional high school student—on important
meeting committees. This official interest in youth has un-
dergone considerable change in the last fifty years of Conservatism, though the records indicate that some of the
great ministers of the past have always had a deep instinct for what is now the official Conservative point of
view regarding the nurture of young people and the value
of young people's service and ideas. Although formerly
quite suspicious of conferences and work camps arranged
in "the will and wisdom of man," all three yearly meetings
have officially encouraged their young people in these
wider Quaker activities since about the time of the Second World War, often providing financial support and
giving time for reports to the yearly meeting and its sub-
ordinate meetings. Their young people have often been active in the YFNA movement, usually in much larger numbers than one would expect from a group of Friends comprising less than one fiftieth of the North American Quaker
population. The degree of loyalty which many young Conservative Friends maintained for Quakerism during the
long years when they were often ignored by the older,
more rigid leadership may possibly be attributed to the
family-like sense of regard between the young and the old
in these close-knit communities (that is, of those who were
willing to remain).

Like other American Friends, the Conservatives have experienced a reviving interest in Quaker education ever since
the Second World War. Like other Friends, they realize
that a powerful force for Quaker cohesion, and for the
gradual, unconscious assimilation of the Quaker way of
life was lost when the one-room Quaker schools ceased to
be practical. Some Conservatives, who instinctively regard
Quakerism as a way of *feeling* and a way of *being* (as well
as a flexible way of believing, and a way of serving), have

begun to search for new ways to provide the environment in which a depth-Quakerism may grow. They are also finding it increasingly necessary to provide intellectual formulations of and justification for their way of life, which on the surface now looks so much like the world around that young people trained in conventional schools may lose touch with—or never find—the inner feel of Quakerism, and may ultimately accept the conventional attitudes about war, etc. It should be emphasized here that most Conservatives are glad that their children have at least some experience in public schools, for they have welcomed this contact with the nation and the world. Where primary schools are being re-established, they are far more competent, far more flexible, and more open to outsiders than the old schools.

The new Conservative meeting at Virginia Beach, Virginia, has recently established a Friends school, adding one grade at a time until it now has seven grades and kindergarten. The other new Conservative meeting in North Carolina, at Durham, plans to begin its school in the same way, having started with kindergarten in 1964. North Carolina Yearly Meeting appoints a Virginia Beach Friends School Committee and devotes about one-sixth of the Yearly Meeting expenditure on the school. Costa Rica Friends established a small primary and secondary school, though some of their children attend Scattergood or Barnesville. The last surviving monthly meeting school of the old style is located near Barnesville, Ohio. Operated by very conservative Somerset Meeting, it usually enrolls fewer than ten pupils.

Although Friends schools will be mentioned in another chapter, it seems important to note the special role played by Scattergood (re-established in 1944) and Olney Friends School (Barnesville) in the life of Conservative Friends. Significantly, these schools are located on farms which help feed and support them, and which are partly operated by students. Scattergood has been unusually successful in combining its study and work programs; Olney does not stress physical work quite so much. Both schools were once rather self-sufficient; at one time Olney even mined its own coal. In spite of changes in the American economy which make such rural self-sufficiency less practical, at least on the hilly land around Barnesville, each school is still a community in itself, carrying on in a less restrictive way the close communities of the Conservative past. There are no day students at either school; even a student whose home is across the road must live in the school. For some Conservative children, even those whose parents have moved away to urban areas, the boarding school is a continuation of the family in the sense that many teachers and students are related to one another or share an intuitive feeling for the Conservative way of life.

However "close" these school communities may seem to some, they have actually been an important source of bringing the world into the two small yearly meetings which support them. Over the years, a stream of teachers, students, and visitors from all over the world has enriched the parent yearly meetings even as it has forced them to re-evaluate their attitudes and practices.

In addition to being important open doors to the world, these schools have long been a significant focus for the energies and love of their members. Many Friends have spent a year or two as teacher or staff member there before embarking on their life work. Because most members have attended these schools, or their children attend, they feel a keen interest in the schools, helping to raise needed money, and often coming for a "work day" at the school. Various Friends have observed that these schools may have been the most important single factor in the survival of these yearly meetings. Budgetary figures give some indication of the affectionate regard in which Conservatives hold their schools. Since Scattergood's re-establishment in 1944, several hundred thousand dollars worth of new buildings have been erected and considerable investment has been made on the school farm. Of course, foundations and friends of the school provided a large measure of the capital funds, but they must have been inspired to this by the heavy support of the largely rural yearly meeting with a membership in 1964 of 780 members (including associates). In 1964 Iowa Yearly Meeting devoted $6,000 of an $8,000 budget to Scattergood. In the same year Ohio Yearly Meeting (845 members) gave $5,000 of its $7,570 budget to Olney.

The new vitality which one can feel in these schools is both a result and a cause of the spirit of Conservative renewal which has developed increasing force since the Second World War. One result of renewal is that at least two of the yearly meetings have re-organized and rewritten their disciplines in modern idiom and with modern psychological insights which leave behind the old judgmental side of traditional Conservatism and its sometimes fearful distance from the world. The new disciplines welcome concern for the world and for participation in wider Quakerism. Like other new disciplines in this century, these attempt to broaden the base of leadership beyond the old order, but, with all of their experiments with rotation of membership on committees, etc., the Conservatives still stress the importance of spirit-led appointments. A visitor to Conservative business meetings and committees will note that they have adopted many of the common-sense efficiency techniques long used by other Friends, but in some cases he may still feel a "slowness" and a tentativeness which sacrifices efficiency because of a search for divine guidance and because of sensitivity to the scruples and hesitations of others. Although it now happens less frequently, committee meetings and even yearly meeting sessions may still be turned, unexpectedly, into meetings for worship at any point in the agenda.

As the old charismatic leadership has declined in numbers and power, and as the close formative environment of the Conservative schools and communities has slowly weakened, the Conservatives have begun to search for new ways to preserve and revitalize the Inner Reality which the old ways were supposed to protect and nurture. They have become more conscious of their history and of the inexorable economic and educational factors which continue to play such a role in their evolution. Most Conservative Friends accordingly see the need for the junior yearly meetings and the Christian education programs which they once spurned. They experiment with workshops, conferences, mid-year meetings and retreats in an effort to recover and gain a deeper understanding of the Reality which their charismatic leaders within living memory had made so real. Examples of this new self-consciousness can be found in North Carolina Yearly Meeting's Visitation Committee, Ohio Yearly Meeting's Spiritual Life Committee, and Iowa Yearly Meeting's Family Placement Committee. The last represents an attempt to help place young families in homes and occupations within reach of Conservative meetings, and it also has helped Iowa Yearly Meeting to recognize that it must adapt to the continuing shift from agricultural communities to the cities. It is perhaps significant that Conservatives in Iowa have been able to establish or to adopt more city meetings than have their brothers in Ohio or North Carolina. This committee has also stressed the importance of helping families moving to non-agricultural meetings to discover new ways of preserving and enriching the kind of family life which makes Conservative Quakerism possible.

Another sign of growing Conservative self-consciousness

was their decision to hold a general meeting at Barnesville in July, 1965. Friends came from as far as California, Florida, and Fritchley, England, to attend the first gathering of this kind ever held. It may be significant that, although it was sponsored by the three surviving Conservative yearly meetings, the gathering was first proposed by a member of New York Yearly Meeting, and that it was attended by several people not members of the Conservative meetings. True to the Conservative ideal of obeying immediate Divine guidance, the general meeting met without any agenda other than hearing answers (prepared and sent in advance by each of the three yearly meetings, Monte Verde Monthly Meeting and Fritchley General Meeting) to nine specially prepared queries on the state of the Society. The brief weekend of sharing revealed the diversity of modern Conservative Quakerism as it struggles to meet the challenges of our day, but it also revealed a common hunger for a living religion of the type experienced by early Friends, whether such religion be described in traditional or modern terms.

As one might expect, the new directions described in this essay are directions only; wide differences can be found among individuals and meetings in the Conservative groups. Among them one may find extremes of activism and quietism, rigidity and openness, provincialism and cosmopolitan alertness. Wide differences in theology may also be found, though the average conservative does tend to agree on the importance and necessity of Divine Guidance, and on the need for depth—regardless of the words used—in worship. A few conservatives may limit their social concerns to the Temperance Committee and the Book Committee, while most of them are increasingly active in other concerns, such as race relations.

Conservatives who have followed these concerns can now be found in many parts of America far from their original meetings. They work for the Service Committee, the FCNL, for Quaker schools and colleges, and in professional positions in the secular world. Surprisingly often a wandering Conservative can find at least one transplanted Conservative in the local meetings he visits.

*   *   *   *

The visitor to the rapidly changing Conservative meetings of today may often sense a spirit of exciting progress rather than the old spirit of continual decay. He will find them more understanding of the causes of their long decline and more hopeful about the future as they consider establishing, adopting, or joining new meetings. In some cases, he will find them very open to all that is good in the modern world, while they retain their deep loyalty (about which visitors often remark) to each other and to their meetings.

UNAFFILIATED FRIENDS MEETINGS
by Isabel N. Bliss

*"A true meeting in the Quaker sense is a meeting
of men which is also a meeting with God."—Pacific
Yearly Meeting Discipline, 1964.*

THE RELIGIOUS SOCIETY OF FRIENDS began as a movement,
and in the unaffiliated groups some of the elements of a
movement remain apparent. There is spontaneity, fluidity,
variety, and experimentation. This small but significant
category is made up of meetings and groups which are not
formally associated in traditional ways with the larger organizations within the Society. This chapter deals briefly with
who and where these Friends are, their general patterns
of development, what they are like, why they are separate, and some of their concerns and contributions.

The traveler looking for Friends Meetings in the United
States would find unaffiliated groups scattered from coast
to coast and from border to border. They range from small
Monthly Meetings whose only formal ties with the Society
are through the Friends World Committee for Consultation to large Yearly Meetings. Some groups of Monthly
Meetings have formed regional associations or conferences
which meet annually without the structure of a Yearly
Meeting. Three Yearly Meetings (Pacific, Southeastern,
and Lake Erie) and two regional groupings (Missouri
Valley Conference and Southern Appalachian Association)
together include eighty-two Monthly and Preparative Meetings and more than twenty informal worship groups.

Most of these unaffiliated groups have been started during the past twenty-five years. In details of history they vary, naturally, but common elements can be found in their development. One underlying factor is the mobility of American people. When Quakers move to an area where no meeting already exists and discover each other, a new group is born. Another factor is the manner of worship. All of the meetings are unprogrammed. The very simplicity of bringing two or three together for quiet waiting upon the Lord invites the experiment.

The typical starting point, then, is the desire for a meeting for worship, which prompts someone to take initiative. West Knoxville, Tenn., says of its beginning, "One family called others to suggest an evening meeting for worship." A meeting in Kansas reports, "One or two individuals were responsible for gathering together several families and individuals who were of the Quaker unprogrammed tradition." This may, indeed, be as far as they ever go, finding satisfaction in meeting more or less regularly after the manner of Friends. At least thirty-three such groups, reaching from Fairbanks, Alaska (Chena Ridge Meeting) to Riverside Church in New York City, are listed by the Friends World Committee.

Those who worship together often find, however, that they share leadings toward joint action. The worship has not taken place in a vacuum, but in a world fraught with tensions, problems, challenges, and opportunities. Friends already well-grounded in the social testimonies are joined by others who are like-minded. There is a feeling of need to organize for greater permanence, effectiveness of action, and mutual strengthening of group and individuals. They wish to act as a unit and as Friends. The traditional step, then, is to request membership in a chosen Yearly Meeting.

There are groups which have felt drawn to the Religious Society of Friends, however, which have not been inclined to make this step. Instead they have taken advantage of the care offered by the American Section of the Friends World Committee for Consultation. By satisfying the conditions set down by that body for new meetings, over sixty groups have been established as Monthly Meetings. The World Committee prefers, nonetheless, that this be an interim arrangement. It encourages the meetings thus established to continue to seek appropriate Yearly Meeting ties. In recent years forty groups recognized by FWCC as Monthly Meetings have joined Yearly Meetings or formed new Yearly Meetings.

Another direction of development is the formation of regional conferences or associations. These are often loosely put together, but fulfill in many respects the need of Monthly Meetings for identification and joint action with a larger group of Friends. The next move beyond the conference or association is the organization of an entirely new Yearly Meeting. The three Yearly Meetings named earlier, Pacific, Southeastern, and Lake Erie, made this transition in 1947, 1962, and 1963 respectively. If any of these should in the future join one of the bodies made up of Yearly Meetings, such as Friends General Conference or Five Years Meeting, they would no longer be unaffiliated Friends!*

Thus we follow the evolution of groups from spontaneous and intimate gatherings for worship through various stages to the fully structured Yearly Meeting. Still we must note that this is not an inevitable process, and there is no standard timing. Groups arise and then disappear; or they have cycles of static periods alternating with spurts of growth and change. Among independent Friends, a diligent inquirer could find examples of groups at each of the stages

---

* South Central Yearly Meeting, with five monthly meetings and two preparative meetings was formed in the same way in 1961, but has since joined the Friends General Conference.

mentioned. The members themselves are in the best position to determine, with God's guidance, the rightness for them of their particular status and directions.

What kinds of Friends are these? I have already referred to some of the characteristics of the groups—relatively new, often small, all unprogrammed. In spite of diversity in make-up and practices, it is still possible to find several other things which they have in common. One is the large proportion of convinced Friends. Most of these meetings report at least fifty percent of their members are not birthright, while some say the percent of convinced Friends is as high as eighty or more. Many of the meetings have grown up near educational centers, drawing their participants from both faculty and students. One correspondent spoke of such a meeting geared to the needs of "modern, educated, sincere seekers." The disciplines and First-day School materials used are usually those of the Friends General Conference. Pacific Yearly Meeting has written its own discipline, and some of the Monthly Meetings have prepared their own queries, advices, and various statements of faith and practice.

The social testimonies play an important part in the life of most unaffiliated meetings. For a number of their members, American Friends Service Commitee programs provided the first contact with the Religious Society of Friends. The AFSC and the Friends Committee on National Legislation are given substantial support by this part of the Society. The two areas of concern and social action most prominent are peace and race relations, although the list of others is long: abolition of capital punishment, fair housing, prison reform, education, civil rights, migrants, and work with foreign students are examples. Sometimes these concerns engage the entire meeting, while at other times they are pursued individually.

Why are these Friends independent? They wish to be a

part of the Religious Society. They share actively in both the spiritual life and social concerns. Yet they refrain from joining the established Yearly Meetings. Why?

There seem to be several answers. First, a distaste for the traditional procedures. In the words of one clerk, "Established Yearly Meetings seemed preoccupied with organizational machinery, with routine reports, too passive, too slow-moving, too formal." Another said, "Many of us did not feel the need for formal organizational 'machinery.' We like the fellowship of like-minded people, but regret the time and money involved in formulating reports, etc."

A second answer is distance. Members of some meetings live several hundred miles from the nearest Yearly Meeting. Lincoln, Nebraska, Friends would have to travel two hundred miles. A Kansas meeting says, "Some members question the need for affiliation over such distances." Meetings in several other states also feel physically isolated.

That mileage does not stand alone as a reason for independence, however, is shown by a closer look at what unaffiliated Friends say on this matter: "No Yearly Meeting of like temper was available geographically" "Distance from any Yearly Meeting with similar points of view." "We would like to affiliate with a Yearly Meeting if one close enough could be found which would meet our needs." Congeniality, then, is important. Young, liberal, unprogrammed and action-oriented groups do not feel immediately at home with older meetings which are predominantly pastoral and rural.

This suggests the dilemma which is inherent in the diversity of American Quakerism. Some meetings were formed when Friends originally belonging to different branches of the Society came together. They manage well enough on a local level, but when affiliation is considered they hesitate to make an exclusive choice for the whole group. Sometimes an unprogrammed meeting will grow up in a com-

munity which already has pastoral and evangelical meetings. Newly convinced members often wish only to get on
with being Quakers—to make a living testimony to which
history and procedural business is quite secondary. By the
same token, new groups may not wish to involve themselves, especially with just one segment of the Society.
Some small groups are not joining simply because they
feel unready or unable to assume the responsibilities.

The evolutionary process still goes on, though, and problems may become opportunities for growth and creative ex-
perimenting. The groups which find "machinery" unap-
pealing are also realizing that there may be merit in the
time-honored procedures when they are rightly used. Lake
Erie is developing a simplified Yearly Meeting structure. A
Colorado meeting writes, "There is active interest in joining a YM as the advantages are well known to us." Another comments, "We acknowledge our debt to traditional
Quakerism."

Members of all branches seem to be growing increasingly uncomfortable with fragmentation within the Society,
and seek for ways of overcoming this. Some of the independent meetings which were unwilling to make a
choice between two larger groups are now exploring how
to join both. "It is possible that when we feel ready to
affiliate it will be with both Friends General Conference
and Five Years Meeting," says someone from Southeastern. Cleveland Meeting is moving toward becoming a
United Meeting with membership in both Lake Erie and
Ohio Conservative Yearly Meetings. Intervisitation, joint
gatherings, and common concerns may lead to new organizational forms. The mutual unreceptiveness of the past
is giving away to willingness to get acquainted (the first
step!), and to openness toward a search together for new
relationships.

What have independent Friends contributed to the Society? For one thing, a common meeting ground. A statement of objectives drawn up in 1955 by the Lake Erie Association said it aimed "To provide a means of bringing together all Friends, regardless of background, into a gathering for worship, fellowship, inspiration, and consideration of common concerns." Lake Erie has rotated the location of its annual meetings to foster contacts with Friends from four branches of the Society. Southeastern Yearly Meeting also sees opportunities to be "a unifying force in the Quaker movement today."

This brings us back to the starting point—the movement. Without overlooking in any way the sustained quality in the life of much of the traditional Society and its members in America today, I feel it can be fairly stated that the new meetings add a fresh and desirable dimension. They grew out of the moving of the spirit of God among them, and sought first of all to gather to worship in His name. They found need to undertake many kinds of loving service to the human family. Unconfined by ready-made forms and undeterred by theological exercises, they have found ways of cultivating the Seed of Truth. Many seekers who come to these meetings, whether as students or in later life, may never actually join the Society of Friends but still their lives are touched in some good way. Though often insecure and sometimes floundering, the new meeting re-lives in an elusive but vital way the experiences of early Christians and early Friends.

What *is* a Friends Meeting, anyway? The answer, the whole answer, does not lie in organizational structure, important as this may be, but in our relation to God. "A true meeting in the Quaker sense," says a paragraph in the Pacific Yearly Meeting Discipline, "is a meeting of men which is also a meeting with God. So far as this divine-human meeting takes place, there is order, unity, and power."

(Note: Inquirers are referred to the American Section, Friends World Committee for Consultation, 152-A North 15th Street, Philadelphia, Pa., 19102, or to the Midwest Office, P.O. Box 38, Plainfield, Indiana, 46168, for information about specific Meetings. A *Friends Directory* listing Meetings for Worship in United States and Canada is published by the Friends World Committee.)

• 7 •

OTHER ASPECTS OF QUAKER OUTREACH

by Edwin B. Bronner

FRIENDS AND EDUCATION

WHILE ALL AMERICAN FRIENDS have a deep interest in education, they do not all believe the same things about it, nor do they carry out similar programs. Some Friends are deeply dedicated to Quaker education, while others who are concerned for public education have little interest in Friends' schools.

The free, or government, or what we call the public schools are very prevalent in much of the United States, while private education is more customary in the Middle Atlantic and New England areas. In regions where virtually all children attend public schools, most Quakers feel that it is important to support such schools and not withdraw from them. Often Friends in such areas provide Quaker colleges for post-secondary education. When Friends began to move west in the nineteenth century they established both elementary schools and academies wherever they went. Gradually these institutions were taken over by the public school system, and very few Friends' schools remain west of the Appalachians.

In the region west of the Mississippi there are only ten Quaker institutions, not counting the Argenta Friends School in British Columbia. These vary from a nursery-kindergarten called Pacific Oaks, near Pasadena, California, to Whittier College which offers a Ph.D. through a cooperative arrangement with neighboring institutions.

There are four boarding schools in this huge area, which makes up nearly two-thirds of the United States, four Quaker colleges, an elementary school, and the afore-mentioned kindergarten. The oldest of these institutions is William Penn College at Oskaloosa, Iowa, founded in 1873 and maintained by Iowa Yearly Meeting (FUM). In the same region Conservative Friends operate Scattergood School at West Branch, Iowa. Kansas Yearly Meeting has strong ties with Friends University, a liberal arts institution at Wichita, and the Friends Bible College and Academy at Haviland, Kansas.

On the West Coast the members of Oregon Yearly Meeting maintain George Fox College as a liberal arts institution with a Christian emphasis, at Newberg, Oregon, and Friends Academy in Greenleaf, Idaho. Whittier College was started by Friends and still has close associations with Quakers, but is not controlled by California Yearly Meeting. With nearly 2,000 students, it is by far the largest institution connected with American Friends. Pacific Yearly Meeting, which was formed in 1947, operates the John Woolman School at Nevada City, California, and its members maintain Pacific Ackworth elementary school in Temple City, California, and the Pacific Oaks kindergarten.

In the region east of the Mississippi, but excluding the confines of New England, New York, and Philadelphia yearly meetings, there are a dozen more Quaker educational institutions. Earlham College, the outstanding institution among this group, was founded in 1847, and achieved collegiate rank in 1859. It is associated with Indiana (FUM) and Western yearly meetings. Indiana also maintains White's Institute at Wabash for underprivileged children. Wilmington Yearly Meeting, in addition to operating the college of the same name known for its work-study program, also maintains Friendsville Academy in Tennessee.

Canadian Friends have an association with Pickering College, a secondary school at Newmarket, Ontario. Members of the newest yearly meeting, Lake Erie, have opened a new school in Detroit, Michigan. Each of the two Ohio yearly meetings maintains a school. The evangelical body operates Malone College at Canton, a liberal arts institution with a strong Christian emphasis, and Conservative Friends support Olney Friends School at Barnesville, a boarding school with a long tradition.

Guilford College, maintained by North Carolina Yearly Meeting, is familiar to all because of the 1967 World Conference. The Conservative Friends of North Carolina operate a school at Virginia Beach, Virginia, and have opened a second in Durham, North Carolina. The Friends of the two Baltimore yearly meetings maintain two schools: Friends School at Baltimore, and the new boarding school at Sandy Springs, Maryland. There is also Sidwell Friends School in Washington, D. C.

In summary, there are twenty-four Quaker educational institutions outside of the three yearly meetings in the northeast, which makes an average of one school for each yearly meeting, for six bodies maintain no school at all. Eight of these institutions are clearly of collegiate rank, and are much like the denominational colleges and universities maintained by Protestant churches all over the United States. Aside from George Fox College, where 60% of the students are Friends, the Quaker colleges are largely serving others. Both Earlham and Guilford attract about twenty percent of their students from Friends, but the other Quaker institutions enroll approximately ten percent Quaker students and the balance from other sources. The two colleges which are closely related to Philadelphia Friends, Haverford and Swarthmore, maintain the same percentage. Only three percent of the Whittier student body is Quaker, and Bryn Mawr College keeps no such record.

The Friends of New England Yearly Meeting maintain five schools, an elementary school at Cambridge, Massachusetts, and four secondary boarding schools. The oldest of these is Moses Brown, a school for boys at Providence, Rhode Island, founded in 1819. The Lincoln School for girls in the same city, is a separate institution, but there is cooperation between the two, not unlike the relationship between Bootham and The Mount in York, England. The Oak Grove School at Vassalboro, Maine, no longer has the close relationship to Friends that it once maintained. Founded in 1957, the Meeting School, at Rindge, New Hampshire, is quite small, and carries on some interesting new ideas in education.

New York Yearly Meeting Friends have just founded an institution called the Friends World College which will include a number of exciting new educational programs in its curriculum. While the headquarters are at Herron Hill on Long Island, portions of the college will meet in other parts of the world. The oldest Friends boarding school in America is the Oakwood School, at Poughkeepsie, founded in 1796 under another name. The Friends Academy at Locust Valley is a secondary school, and the Westbury Friends School, on Long Island, is a kindergarten. In the New York City area Friends have two large day schools which enroll both elementary and secondary students, Brooklyn Friends, and Friends Seminary.

The schools maintained by Friends of Philadelphia Yearly Meeting are too numerous to mention individually, for they include twenty-four pre-school and elementary schools, eight institutions which include both elementary and secondary schools, two boarding schools and three colleges. Philadelphia Yearly Meeting was divided into two separate bodies from 1827 until 1955, and this is one reason for the large number of schools. Westtown School, founded in 1799, was kept by the Orthodox at the time of the separation, and the Quakers of that same branch founded Haverford College in 1833. The Friends of Philadelphia Yearly Meeting (Race) chartered Swarthmore College in 1864, and they opened George School as a boarding school late in the nineteenth century. Competition between the two colleges, and the two boarding schools, is lively today, but there are no longer any theological lines drawn between them. Haverford is for men only, while Swarthmore and the boarding schools are co-educational. Bryn Mawr College, founded by Friends in 1885 as a woman's college, has only loose ties with Quakers today, but cooperates closely with Haverford on educational matters.

Several of the schools are in New Jersey, including co-educational day schools for the twelve grades at Atlantic City and Moorestown, and there is a similar school in Wilmington, Delaware. The largest of the institutions in Pennsylvania is Germantown Friends, with more than 700 students. The oldest are William Penn Charter and Friends Select, both in Philadelphia, which date their beginnings from 1689. The other two day schools which combine both elementary and secondary programs are Abington Friends and Friends Central, both on the outskirts of Philadelphia. All of the Friends schools in the Philadelphia area welcome non-Quakers, and only in George School and Westtown are Friends students in a majority. This means that Quaker education has an influence far beyond the confines of the Society of Friends.

There are several centers for study in various parts of the United States, but the oldest and best known is Pendle Hill. Founded in 1930, it grew out of an earlier center called Woolman School, which existed between 1915 and 1927. Similar to Woodbrooke, in England, Howard Brinton once referred to it as a "center for study, a place of work and worship, a Quaker experiment in community." It has made a major contribution to Quaker thought through the Pendle Hill Pamphlets and other publications. Since it always includes international students and faculty in the program, Pendle Hill has influenced Quakerism around the world. Located at Wallingford, outside of Philadelphia, it operates on a term basis, corresponding to the four seasons, but with the summer session much shorter than the other three terms.

Many yearly meetings have committees which are concerned with Quaker education, and there is a national body, the Friends Council on Education, founded in 1931, and located in Philadelphia, which serves as an advisory and consultative body. The Quaker College Presidents also have a loose organization which meets annually.

AMERICAN FRIENDS SERVICE COMMITTEE [*]

The A.F.S.C. was organized on April 30, 1917 by Friends representing several areas of American Quakerism. They were deeply concerned for the spiritual values endangered by America's entrance into the War, and they also wanted to provide constructive, non-military services for the young men who were conscientious objectors.

The British Friends War Victims Relief Committee, already working in France, included American Quakers in its relief and reconstruction efforts, and six Quaker women joined British workers in Russia.

When the peace treaty was signed in the summer of 1919, and it was possible to enter Germany, the A.F.S.C., at

---

[*] Prepared by the Information Service, AFSC.

Herbert Hoover's request, undertook a large German child-feeding operation. Relief work was carried on in Austria and Poland, and a famine relief program in Russia was undertaken.

The red and black star (first used as a symbol by British Friends on relief missions during the Franco-Prussian War of 1870) was to become a familiar sign in more parts of the world than anyone could foresee at the time of this small beginning. Following the war, a basic work of reconciliation through Friends International Centers developed in more than a dozen cities around the world. At the same time, the Committee at home found hundreds of young people volunteering their services as they became aware of the vast needs here. Work in coal mines, self-help housing projects, the early work camps, peace caravans, work in Mexico—all had their beginnings as emergency needs abroad decreased.

Behind these developments was a recognition that relief of suffering was a proper witness to Friends' deepest convictions but that alone it was not enough. The violences and injustices which created the need for relief were evidences of deep social ills and moral insensitivities. To undertake relief without seeking to tackle the causes of suffering was to ignore half of the task. So came "peace education" work and programs concerned with racial and economic justice. Then, with the outbreak of the Spanish Civil War in 1937, and in the midst and in the wake of World War II, the Committee's relief services grew once more, moving through France, Finland, Italy, Germany, Austria, Poland, Hungary, and eastward to India, China, and Japan. By the end of 1946, the Committee's budget called for seven million dollars for relief alone. In the United States, conscientious objection brought 3,400 men into camps and units administered by AFSC.

The work of the Service Committee today is organized

into five program divisions that reflect concerns and testimonies shared widely among American Friends.

The International Service Division attempts to bind up the wounds of war and to help those who have suffered to begin life anew. Refugee work among the Hungarians, Arabs, Cubans, and Chinese has been a major part of its program. Thousands of Friends are among those who continue to contribute to relief needs, and this is probably the best-known part of AFSC work. Projects to help free man from hunger and disease also come under this section as does assistance in family planning and community development. Such work is a vital part of its total service, but the Committee does not feel justified in being merely a large-scale relief organization. It attempts to prevent the violence that brings man such suffering.

The International Affairs Division works to open, to renew, and to deepen communications among men who differ in nationality, culture, ideology, or moral codes. Believing in the message of Jesus that love is the great reconciling power, the AFSC seeks to create conditions in which men may openly discuss their differences and go about solving them in a spirit of reconciliation. This is the broad purpose of the Quaker United Nations Program, the conferences for diplomats, the international student seminars, and the seminars in Washington with members of the Administration and of Congress.

The Youth Services Division provides opportunities for young people to test their ideals in practical work with others at home and abroad. As the young volunteers work with and not for others, they learn what love for others really means, and they often come to a sense of God's purpose for them in the world. In seminars, conferences, and institutes, young people learn of the barriers of race and ideology that divide men, and often find what a spirit of reconciliation can do to overcome these conflicts.

Underlying the work of the Community Relations Division is the call of Jesus for men to love one another. The AFSC believes that if this call is to mean anything in the world today, it must be woven into the complex social fabric in which all men live. This means work for integrated schools and housing, for employment on merit rather than color, for solutions to some of the difficult problems of migrant laborers and American Indians.

Through its Peace Education Division, AFSC proclaims the Quaker testimony that peace on earth must be worked for as well as prayed for. To make known the truth that war is wrong is perhaps the largest challenge. The division works through literature, institutes, seminars, and family camps, and with Friends' churches and meetings, other churches, and a variety of other groups.

The executive secretary and his immediate associates coordinate the work of the Committee. However, it is the Corporation, comprising more than 200 Friends from 20 yearly meetings and two Friends' associations, that constitutes the legal entity of the AFSC; and it is the Board of Directors of 55 members—all of them Friends, each selected by the Corporation from its own membership—that determines AFSC policy. The five program divisions are serviced by five central departments—accounting, the business office, the information and publications service, personnel, and fund raising.

In the international aspects of many of its programs, the AFSC works in cooperation with the Friends Service Council of London and Ireland Yearly Meetings. However, the AFSC does not represent officially any Yearly Meeting within the Society of Friends and does not speak for the Society.

Since the spirit and effectiveness of AFSC programs depend on the quality of its staff members, the personnel department searches constantly for dedicated people among

Friends and other religiously motivated persons who share the concerns of Friends. Of the 24 persons responsible for executive action in the national and regional offices, 21 are Friends. In the total administrative and field staff, national, regional, and overseas, the percentage of Friends ranges between 40 percent and 60 percent. In view of the small size of the Society of Friends, these figures are significant. To finance its programs the AFSC welcomes gifts from all who want to give their financial and moral support to its work.

FRIENDS COMMITTEE ON NATIONAL LEGISLATION

With the coming of the Second World War, Friends in the United States realized that they needed some organization, some method of joining together to make an impact upon the national government. When London Yearly Meeting, or its Meeting for Sufferings, makes a statement in Britain, the government recognizes the fact that this represents, substantially, the view of Quakers in the country. With some two dozen separate Friends bodies in the United States, no united Quaker voice was apparent in Washington. Separate yearly meetings could issue statements, address letters to government officials, and on rare occasions send a person to speak to men in the capital, but this was not enough.

Thus it was that a group of Friends gathered at Quaker Hill, in Richmond, Indiana, in 1943, to organize what is called the Friends Committee on National Legislation. It was agreed that a national committee would meet periodically to discuss issues, make decisions, and set the policy of the program. The staff of the FCNL does not take a position on any issue without the approval of the Committee. While it has been recognized from the beginning that the FCNL does not speak for all Friends in the United States, it is equally clear that a majority of American Quakers believe in and support the ideas advanced by the Committee and its staff.

Three persons gathered in a makeshift office in the Florida Avenue meetinghouse in Washington, D. C., in November, 1943, and the Quaker lobby was launched. The first Executive Secretary of the Committee was E. Raymond Wilson, who has spearheaded the work for two decades, and is still active even though serving in an emeritus status. Jeanette Hadley, who began work with the Committee at the same time, is still active as Assistant Secretary. The present Executive Secretary of the FCNL is Edward F. Snyder, who joined the staff in 1955. While there were only three persons on the payroll of the Committee in 1943, the staff has been greatly enlarged over the years, and the annual budget of the Committee is now some $100,000.

Initially the FCNL was deeply involved in issues connected with the war, such as the rights of conscientious objectors and the problems of relief and reconstruction. It soon broadened its concerns to include many issues related to peace and human brotherhood. In addition to presenting Quaker views to members of Congress and other government officials, through personal interviews, testimony before Congressional committees, and printed statements, the FCNL turned to other efforts.

A Newsletter about affairs in Washington was started very early in the career of the Committee, and has been sent on a monthly basis to thousands of persons, Friends and non-Friends, who were interested in learning more about what was happening in the nation's capital. The Newsletter, the Action bulletins, and other printed material have provided the background for Quakers in all parts of the country, and have served as a basis for letter writing campaigns, concerted efforts to visit Congressmen either in Washington or when they were home, and for the education and enlightenment of local Friends meetings.

The FCNL also began to sponsor conferences, seminars and other gatherings for farmers, ministers, young people, and other groups of Friends and some non-Friends. Prominent government officials were invited to speak, fruitful discussions were held, and visits to government departments, embassies of foreign countries, and the halls of Congress, have been a part of these projects. Quaker colleges and secondary schools have obtained much assistance from the FCNL over the years, during visits to Washington, in connection with courses in the schools, and in other ways. Members of the staff have visited a great many of the Friends meetings in America to bring the concerns of the FCNL before local groups and individuals.

Over the years the Friends Committee on National Legislation has taken a leading role in the fight against universal military training, it has supported efforts to strengthen the United Nations, it has worked steadily for disarmament, and it has been most active in seeking new ways to guarantee international peace. It has contributed to the campaign to change the immigration laws of the United States, has worked for better Civil Rights legislation, and has maintained the traditional concern for improving the conditions of American Indians. The FCNL played a vital role in securing the passage of the Peace Corps legislation and in the establishment of the Arms Control and Disarmament Agency, and has been an important link in the Food for Peace program.

The FCNL has always made its position regarding issues before the Congress very clear, and its spokesmen have gained the respect of legislators even when they have not agreed with them. It has gathered the facts needed to bring about the passage of some laws, and always attempts to present complete, straightforward, honest testimony when the opportunity arises.

In three regions of the United States local Friends operate area offices on legislative matters. These are entirely independent of the FCNL, but there is a good deal of informal cooperation. These offices, two in California, and the other in Chicago, divide their time and effort between the national scene, and the political arena of the region. Some effective work on the abolition of capital punishment and the care of the mentally ill has been done at the state level by these offices.

The FCNL offices at 245 Second Street, N.E., Washington, D. C., 20002, are just behind the new Senate Office Building, and convenient to all of the legislative buildings on Capitol Hill.

FRIENDS WORLD COMMITTEE, AMERICAN SECTION

The Friends World Committee for Consultation was formed in 1937 following the World Conference which gathered that year at Swarthmore and Haverford colleges. There has been an American Section, as well as a European Section from the early days, and now a strong effort is being made to create an active African Section as well.

For many years the American Section of the FWCC existed alongside the American Friends Fellowship Council which was formed in 1936. This body was created to encourage and support new Friends meetings in areas where existing yearly meetings were unable to meet the needs of such Friends. It also sponsored the Wider Quaker Fellowship, originated by Rufus Jones as a fellowship of persons who wished to be associated with Friends even though continuing formal relations with other religious organizations.

Since 1954 when the two combined under the official name, Friends World Committee for Consultation, American Section and Fellowship Council, the programs of the two organizations have been merged. The purposes of the American Section can best be summarized in five short paragraphs. Four of these were formulated at the FWCC meeting in Oxford, England, in 1952, after the third world conference. The fifth (number 4 as quoted here) was added at a meeting of the FWCC Interim Committee in October 1965.

1) To encourage and strengthen the spiritual life within the Society of Friends through such measures as the promotion of intervisitation, study, conferences and a wide sharing of experience on the deepest spiritual level.

2) To help Friends to gain a better understanding of the world-wide character of the Society of Friends and its vocation in the world today.

3) To promote consultation amongst Friends of all cultures, countries and languages. The Committee seeks to bring the different groups of Friends into intimate touch with one another on the basis of their common Quaker heritage, with a view to sharing experience and coming to some measure of agreement in regard to their attitude to modern world problems.

4) To promote understanding between Friends of all countries and members of other branches of the Christian Church and members of other religious faiths, and to interpret the specific Quaker message to those who seek for further religious experience.

5) To keep under review the Quaker contribution in world affairs and to facilitate both the examination and presentation of Quaker thinking and concern.

The American Section maintains two offices, one in

Philadelphia, and the other in the mid-west. The mid-western office was at Wilmington, Ohio, from 1954-1964, and has been at Plainfield, Indiana, since that time.

The FWCC as a Non-Governmental Organization with consultative status at the United Nations, has a staff in New York with the dual purpose of working closely with the men and women of the United Nations, and also interpreting the work of the UN to Quakers. The mid-west office of the FWCC, American Section, has made an important contribution to this second goal. The administrative responsibilities for the Quaker UN program are provided by the American Friends Service Committee in cooperation with corresponding bodies in the British Isles.

Twenty-four yearly meetings in the western hemisphere, and the General Meeting in Mexico, belong to the American Section, and share actively in the concerns and projects which Friends undertake through this organization. Representatives of most of these bodies gather together for the annual meeting which is held in different parts of the United States. The semi-annual meetings are sometimes held outside the U.S.

Through visitation, publications, interpretive materials and conferences, the FWCC, American Section, seeks to advance the purposes of Friends. It has also sponsored conferences on race relations, the treatment of prisoners, civil liberties, and peace. It attempts to fill the needs of Friends which are not provided for by other existing Quaker organizations.

BIOGRAPHICAL NOTES

ISABEL N. BLISS, a member of Cleveland Monthly Meeting, has been active in the Committee on Greater Unity in Ohio. She has great interest in the Friends group in Korea.

EDWIN B. BRONNER, is Professor of History and Curator of the Quaker Collection at Haverford College. He is chairman of the Planning Committee for the Friends World Conference in 1967.

LAWRENCE McK. MILLER, General Secretary of the Friends General Conference, is now in India with his family with the VISA program of the American Friends Service Committee.

ARTHUR O. ROBERTS, Professor of Religion and Philosophy at George Fox College, is editor of *Concern,* the publication of the Friends Evangelical Association.

DAVID O. STANFIELD, is Secretary of Stewardship and Finance for the Friends United Meeting.

WILLIAM P. TABER, JR., a member of Ohio Yearly Meeting (Conservative), was formerly Headmaster of the Friends Boarding School, Barnesville, Ohio, and is currently a T. Wistar Brown Fellow at Haverford College.

Religious Society of Friends in U.S.A., Canada, and Mexico

Friends United Meeting

Alaska	1,500
Baltimore	1,212
California	7,515
Canadian*	404
Indiana	13,206
Iowa	5,670
Mexico (1962 data)	197
Nebraska	373
New England*	1,641
New York*	3,352
North Carolina	14,837
Western	12,410
Wilmington	4,367
	66,684

Friends General Conference

Baltimore	2,230
Canadian*	403
Illinois	1,034
Indiana	746
New England*	1,641
New York*	3,353
Philadelphia	17,313
South Central	290
Green Pastures Quarterly Mtg., Lake Erie Y.M.	204
	27,214

Evangelical Friends Alliance

Kansas	8,119
Ohio	8,037
Oregon	5,915
Rocky Mountain	1,561
	23,632

Conservative Friends

Iowa	736
North Carolina	136
Ohio	845
	1,717

Unaffiliated Meetings

Lake Erie Y.M.	467
Pacific Y.M.	1,486
Southeastern Y.M.	395
Other meetings	649
	2,997
Central Y.M.	501
Total	122,745

* Since these Yearly Meetings belong to both FUM and FGC, membership has been divided.

Figures provided by FWCC, American Section. Data for 1964.

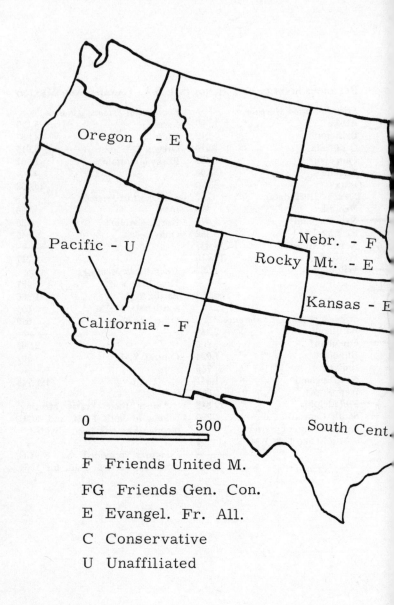

Oregon - E

Pacific - U

Nebr. - F

Rocky Mt. - E

California - F

Kansas - E

0   500

South Cent.

F   Friends United M.

FG Friends Gen. Con.

E   Evangel. Fr. All.

C   Conservative

U   Unaffiliated

Canad.
- F/FG

New Eng.
- F/FG

N. Y.

Lake Erie - U   F/FG

Phila.   FG

wa - F & C

Ind.   F & FG

Ohio E & C   Balt. F & FG

Ill. - FG

West. F   Wilm. F

No. Carol. - F & C

FG

Southeast - U